HOW LYNDON B. JOHNSON FOUGHT THE VIETNAM WAR

PRESIDENTS AT WAR

HOW LYNDON B. JOHNSON FOUGHT THE VIETNAM WAR

Jason Porterfield

Enslow Publishing
101 W. 23rd Street
Suite 240
New York, NY 10011
USA
enslow.com

Published in 2018 by Enslow Publishing, LLC.
101 W. 23rd Street, Suite 240, New York, NY 10011

Library of Congress Cataloging-in-Publication Data

Names: Porterfield, Jason, author.
Title: How Lyndon B. Johnson fought the Vietnam War / Jason Porterfield.
Description: New York, NY : Enslow Publishing, 2018. | Series: Presidents at war | Includes bibliographical references and index. | Audience: Grades 7–12.
Identifiers: LCCN 2017007006 | ISBN 9780766085312 (library bound)
Subjects: LCSH: Johnson, Lyndon B. (Lyndon Baines), 1908–1973—Military leadership—Juvenile literature. | Vietnam War, 1961–1975—United States—Juvenile literature. | Presidents—United States—Biography—Juvenile literature. | United States—Politics and government—1963–1969—Juvenile literature. | United States—Foreign relations—1963–1969—Juvenile literature.
Classification: LCC E847.2 .P67 2018 | DDC 973.923092—dc23
LC record available at https://lccn.loc.gov/2017007006

Printed in the United States of America

To Our Readers: We have done our best to make sure all website addresses in this book were active and appropriate when we went to press. However, the author and the publisher have no control over and assume no liability for the material available on those websites or on any websites they may link to. Any comments or suggestions can be sent by e-mail to customerservice@enslow.com.

Photo Credits: Cover, pp. 1, 3, 7, 10, 23, 35, 47, 56, 68, 87, 100, 109 LBJ Library photo by Arnold Newman; cover, p. 3 Keystone-France/Gamma-Keystone/Getty Images; pp. 8, 11, 29, 33, 48, 91, 93 Bettmann/Getty Images; pp. 14, 17, 42 © AP Images; p. 24 Ruslan Olinchuk/Alamy Stock Photo; p. 26 Wolfgang Kaehler/LightRocket/Getty Images; p. 37 Alfred Eisenstaedt/The LIFE Picture Collection/Getty Images; p. 44 Photo12/Universal Images Group/Getty Images; p. 51 PhotoQuest/Archive Photos/Getty Images; p. 58 Francis Miller/The LIFE Picture Collection/Getty Images; p. 69 Tim Page/Corbis Historical/Getty Images; p. 74 Hulton Archive/Getty Images; p. 79 Corbis Historical/Getty Images; p. 83 CBS Photo Archive/Getty Images; p. 89 Keystone/Hulton Archive/Getty Images; p. 101 John Olson/The LIFE Images Collection/Getty Images; p. 103 dikobraziy/Shutterstock.com; p. 108 nik wheeler/Corbis Historical/Getty Images; p. 110 Education Images/Universal Images Group/Getty Images.

CONTENTS

INTRODUCTION 7

CHAPTER 1 GROWING INTO POLITICS 10

CHAPTER 2 A NATION IN CONFLICT 23

CHAPTER 3 ESCALATION IN ASIA 35

CHAPTER 4 ASSESSING VIETNAM 47

CHAPTER 5 THE MIDDLE COURSE 56

CHAPTER 6 SHIFTING MOMENTUM 68

CHAPTER 7 SPINNING OUT OF CONTROL 87

CHAPTER 8 PASSING THE BATON 100

CONCLUSION 109

CHRONOLOGY 112

CHAPTER NOTES 116

GLOSSARY 123

FURTHER READING 125

INDEX 126

INTRODUCTION

In the decades following the end of World War II (1939–1945), the United States and the Union of Soviet Socialist Republics (Soviet Union) were locked in a struggle to spread their own forms of government to other parts of the world. The Soviet Union wanted to expand its influence by helping to spread communism. The US worked to keep it in check by helping to set up young democracies. This bloodless struggle was called the Cold War, and it lasted from 1947 until the collapse of the Soviet Union in 1991.

The Soviet Union and the United States never fought each other directly, but took opposing sides in many smaller struggles. During the 1950s, the two nations became involved in a struggle that started out as a war for independence and then turned into a civil war in the divided Southeast Asian nation of Vietnam. What began as the US sending funds and military advisors eventually evolved into a full-scale war.

Texas-born Lyndon Baines Johnson (1908–1973) was president of the United States from 1963 to 1969, the years during which the US became deeply involved in Vietnam.

He oversaw the development of the US military's strategy in the war. Reluctant to fully commit to the war but believing it was necessary to prevent communism from spreading throughout Asia, he sent hundreds of thousands of soldiers into Vietnam even after things began going badly.

Lyndon Johnson speaks with reporters outside the LBJ Ranch in Johnson City, Texas. Johnson's presidency was marked by the Vietnam War and social upheaval.

Ultimately, the war became one of the longest and costliest conflicts in US history. It cost the lives of more than 58,000 US soldiers, as well as millions of Vietnamese soldiers and civilians. Tensions over the war and race relations in the US boiled over into protests and even riots during Johnson's presidency as the fighting continued.

Johnson's legacy as president is largely defined by Vietnam and his inability to get the US out of the war. He was much more than that. A skilled politician, he used his energy and charisma to rise to positions of power in the Senate. A plain-speaking and physically imposing man, he was able to effectively charm, prod, and bully his colleagues into passing important civil rights legislation. When he became president, he used these same skills to push through more effective civil rights laws and important social programs designed to help lift people out of poverty.

The war that he failed to avoid lasted beyond his presidency and did not end until after his death in 1973. Even now, his war plans and US strategies in Vietnam are studied as experts work to understand how the US fell short of defeating a much more poorly equipped fighting force.

GROWING INTO POLITICS

Lyndon Baines Johnson was born on August 27, 1908, in Stonewall, Texas. He was the oldest child of Rebekah Baines Johnson and Samuel Ealy Johnson, Jr. The couple would later have one more son—Sam Houston Johnson—and three daughters—Rebekah, Josefa, and Lucia.

The Johnson family lived on a small ranch near the Pedernales River. The Johnson and Baines families had deep roots in that part of Texas. Rebekah Baines Johnson's grandfather was a Baptist minister who founded several churches in the area and went on to become president of Baylor University. Her father, Joseph Wilson Baines, served in the Texas state legislature and was secretary of state under Texas governor John Ireland. Before marrying, she studied literature at Baylor University, worked as an elocution teacher and wrote articles for local newspapers.

On his father's side, a cousin was the namesake of a nearby small town called Johnson City. No matter where his career took him, Lyndon Johnson would maintain a strong connection to the region throughout his life.

The Johnson home was so small that the children had to share beds. After the family moved away, Lyndon Johnson's aunt bought the house and added rooms.

The Johnson family sometimes struggled for money. Samuel Johnson had worked as a barber and a schoolteacher before becoming serious about working his family's farm. The farm was successful, but he lost money by speculating on the price of cotton and ended up deeply in debt be the time Lyndon was a teenager.[1]

The Johnsons were a political family. Samuel Johnson's father, Samuel Ealy Johnson, Sr., was a member of the Texas State Legislature. In 1904, Samuel Johnson decided to follow in his father's and his father-in-law's footsteps was elected to the Texas House of Representatives. He served there for six terms. Though he was a successful politician, his luck as a farmer and businessman did not improve and he lost the family farm in 1906. Lyndon Johnson later remembered his as impoverished, but happy. Like many homes in the rural United States at that time, the Johnson home did not have electricity or running water. The poverty that the family experienced made a deep impression on him.

The Johnson family moved to Johnson City in 1913, as Samuel Johnson finally gave up farming. Lyndon Johnson entered Johnson City High School as an indifferent student. He was obviously intelligent, but was uninterested in doing the work necessary to do well in his classes. Still, he made three-mile trip in to town on a mule every day so that he could attend classes. He was very close to his mother, who saw his potential and encouraged him to work harder at his studies. Although his grades did not improve dramatically, he made his mark in other ways. Like his father, he was very outgoing and made friends easily. By the time he graduated in 1924, he had played baseball, edited the school newspaper, and was captain of a school debate team that made it all the way to the state finals. He was even elected president of his senior class, which consisted of six students.[2]

The Road to College

Lyndon had decided at an early age that he wanted to do something with his life outside of agriculture. The Johnson family had worked hard to get him into summer classes at Southwest Texas State Teachers College (now Texas State University—San Marcos), but his grades were poor and the college did not admit him after he graduated from high school. He left Texas for a short time and worked at odd jobs in California before returning home.

He was more serious about his studies when he finally enrolled at Southwest Texas State Teachers College in 1927, with the intention of becoming a teacher. He held several jobs at the college while he attended classes, including serving as an office assistant and working as a janitor. Lyndon also continued some of his high school interests. He was a member of the debate team and was elected to serve in the student government. He also edited the college newspaper.

As part of his training to become a teacher, he accepted an assignment to teach in the town of Catulla. The school there was very small, not unlike the one-room schools Lyndon himself had attended as a boy. The students were all Hispanic and lived in deep poverty. In addition to being their teacher, he was also the school's principal. He worked hard to inspire his students to do their best. Lyndon taught there for two years and earned praise for his work from other teachers and from people in Catulla. Working in the town also had a profound effect on him. The poverty that he encountered there was even deeper than what he had experienced as a child. The lives that his students led inspired him to dedicate his life to doing his best to end poverty.[3]

Lyndon graduated from Southwest Texas State Teachers College in 1930. He took a job teaching English and public speaking at Sam Houston High School in Houston, Texas. Lyndon had a gift for teaching and again won praise for his hard work. The Great Depression (1929–1939) had taken hold in much of the country and he saw the effect

Lyndon Johnson stands alongside three other teachers at the elementary school where he taught in Cotulla, Texas.

"I often walked home late in the afternoon after the classes were finished wishing there was more that I could do. But all I knew was to teach them the little that I knew, hoping that I might help them against the hardships that lay ahead.

And somehow you never forget what poverty and hatred can do when you see its scars on the hopeful face of a young child."[4]

it had on his students. As in Catulla, many of his students at Sam Houston High were Hispanic and poor. They also faced discrimination because of their ethnicity. Some spoke mostly Spanish, a language that Lyndon learned so that he could communicate with them, He encouraged his students to develop their English skills so that they would have an easier time outside of their community. He coached the school's debate team. He would later become known in Texas as a champion of Hispanic people.

Getting Started in Politics

Lyndon also became involved in politics for the first time while he lived in Houston, cutting his teaching career short. His family had a long history of political involvement on both sides. Lyndon himself would later remember telling a fellow grade school classmate that he would grow up to become president.[5]

Lyndon's father was still involved with the Democratic Party and had many friends in Texas politics. One such friend was a powerful rancher named Richard Kleberg. In 1931, Kleberg decided to run for an open seat in the US House of Representatives. Lyndon volunteered to work on his campaign. Kleberg won the election easily. He repaid Lyndon for his hard work by offering him a job. He wanted Lyndon to join him in Washington, DC, and work as an aide in his office. Accepting the job would mean leaving his home in Texas behind, but working on the campaign helped Lyndon rediscover his political ambitions. He accepted and accompanied Kleberg to the nation's capital.

As a congressional aide, he took care of many of the behind-the-scenes duties that Kleberg could not handle on his own. Lyndon showed himself to have a boundless energy for helping Kleberg. He answered letters that came into the office from Kleberg's constituents. Many were suffering from widespread drought. Lyndon made many calls to government agencies in order to get financial help for them. He had a take charge attitude even at that early stage in his political career.

Lyndon researched pending legislation, learning the ins and outs of proposed laws so that he could advise Kleberg on whether to vote for or against them. Kleberg quickly came to rely on Johnson's energy and intelligence. When Kleberg traveled back to Texas to take care of business in his district, Lyndon would join him.

Lyndon met his future wife, Claudia "Lady Bird" Taylor, during one of those trips to the Texas capital at Austin. She was a recent college graduate, with a degree in journalism and a teaching certificate. Lyndon asked her out on a date, beginning a whirlwind courtship that ended in marriage just three months later, in November of 1934. They remained married until Lyndon's death in 1973 and had two daughters, Lynda in 1944 and Luci in 1947. During his long political career, Lady Bird Johnson's friendliness and gracious manners often countered her husband's sometimes gruff personality.[6]

Lyndon's hard work in Kleberg's office soon paid off. President Franklin Roosevelt noticed Lyndon's work ethic and offered him another kind of job. Roosevelt knew Lyndon's background was in education and working with children. In 1935, Roosevelt appointed Lyndon to serve as Texas's Director of the National Youth Administration.

Lyndon and Lady Bird Johnson pose at the US Capitol building shortly after their wedding. Lady Bird's investment in a Texas radio station helped fund Lyndon Johnson's first election.

Johnson secured the position with the help of the powerful Texas Congressman Sam Rayburn, who recommended Johnson for the job. The National Youth Administration was one of Roosevelt's "New Deal" projects designed to provide jobs to millions of people who had been thrown out of work by the Great Depression. Under Johnson's leadership, the NYA worked to help people age sixteen to twenty-five find jobs. It also provided education, training, and counseling to young women and men who were unemployed. In one of the NYA's programs, students who stayed in school were given small payments in exchange for part-time work. The money could make a huge difference to Texas families, especially farmers who were hit hard by droughts.

Johnson led the program successfully until 1937, providing aid to desperately poor people. He made many important political contacts in his position and developed a loyal staff. That year, one of Texas's seats in the US House of Representatives opened up when US Representative James Buchanan died suddenly. Buchanan had been the representative of Johnson's home congressional district, and Lyndon saw an opportunity. Johnson consulted with his political allies and decided that the time was right to take his first shot at running for office.[7]

Johnson had never run for office before, but he had worked on campaigns and knew how to get results. He paid his campaign expenses with funds that Lady Bird Johnson had inherited, along with money she earned from owning a Texas radio station. He used his involvement with the NYA and his support for Roosevelt's New Deal policies to win over voters. The campaign was successful and he won the seat, beating six other candidates. He was only twenty-eight when he was elected.[8]

Johnson stayed in the House of Representatives for the next decade. His record as a US Representative was mixed during his first years. He remained very ambitious, and in 1941 he ran for an open senate seat and lost. He fulfilled his commitment to the people of his Texas district by helping to bring electricity to the region, as well as federal money

Volunteering for War

In his 1941 Senate campaign, Johnson promised voters that if the country went to war, he would enlist in the military. He swore that he wouldn't take a safe desk job—he'd fight the enemy on the battlefield. On December 10, 1941—three days after the Japanese bombed Pearl Harbor—Johnson was ordered to report for active duty, becoming the first member of Congress to volunteer. Johnson was not sent overseas during his first few months of service, but in April 1942, he was assigned to a survey team in the war zone in the Pacific. On June 9, Johnson accompanied a bomber mission in which his plane was forced to turn back due to mechanical trouble while under enemy fire. He was awarded the Army Silver Star Medal for his actions. Johnson's military stint ended shortly afterwards, when a July 9 directive from President Roosevelt required the return of all national legislators in the armed services.[9]

for housing projects and for building dams that would help farmers. He was popular in the district and was easily reelected in every election up through 1948.

Senate Mastery

Johnson made another push to enter the Senate in 1948. Even though he was still popular in his district, he had a harder time winning support in the statewide race. His opponent for the Democratic Party's nomination was Texas Governor Coke Stevenson, who was very popular throughout the state. Johnson's commitment to Roosevelt's New Deal had helped him win votes in previous elections.

By 1949, however, the economy was in much better shape and many Americans had turned against the social programs. The US was in the early days of the Cold War with the Soviet Union, which had a communist government. Opponents of the New Deal believed that the government-funded programs were too close to communism and that they would help spread communist beliefs. Johnson had also made some shrewd financial investments during World War II. His opponents accused him of using his position in the House of Representatives to profit from the war.

The race between Johnson and Stevenson turned out to be extremely close, with Johnson beating Stevenson by only eighty-seven votes before going on to easily win the general election. Many decades later, the historian and Robert A. Caro uncovered evidence showing that Johnson's campaign had actually created thousands of fraudulent votes in order to help him win. The outcome showed Johnson's willingness to do whatever it took to win.[10]

Johnson quickly rose through the Senate's leadership ranks. He became the majority whip for the Senate Democrats in 1950. It became his job to make sure that all of the party's senators were present for votes and that they voted according to the party's policies. Just two years later, in 1952, the Senate Democrats elected him to the position of Minority Leader. In this role, he set the party's direction in terms of how members would vote and which legislation they would support.

Johnson's ability to work with Democrats from across the country helped boost him to his leadership roles. He also developed a good working relationship with President Dwight Eisenhower, who was a Republican. In 1955, the Democrats became the majority party in the senate, and Johnson became majority leader despite suffering from a serious heart attack that year. He was still in his first term.

The Democratic Party was deeply divided at that time. Jim Crow laws, which were laws that specifically discriminated against African Americans and other minorities, were in effect in many states. In southern states such as Texas, these racist laws were a cornerstone of politics. African Americans were often denied the right to vote, were forced to live in certain neighborhoods, had to attend separate schools from white children, and suffered many other indignities. They were also often subjected to violence and abuse from white racists. Within the federal government, a powerful group of senators from the south called the Southern Caucus worked to block civil rights laws that would have guaranteed rights for non-white citizens. Northern Democrats were not as supportive of Jim Crow laws as their southern colleagues and often differed with the Southern Caucus. Early in his senate career, Johnson allied himself with the Southern Caucus. As a representative, he had voted against civil rights legislation that would have eased discrimination against African Americans.[11]

Johnson had begun his break from the Southern Caucus in 1954, when he refused to sign a pledge to resist the racial integration of public schools. He was majority leader when President Eisenhower proposed a tough civil rights bill that included strong measures to guarantee that it would be enforced. Johnson knew that it was important to pass a civil rights bill, but he also realized that the Southern Caucus would block passage of the bill that Eisenhower envisioned. He managed to lead the senate to pass a weaker version of the bill, but even that effort was a struggle. He spent the next few years working to strengthen the Democratic Party, making alliances with newly elected northern Democrats, and preparing to enter the 1960 presidential campaign.[12]

A NATION IN CONFLICT

It has often been said that the Americans and the Vietnamese viewed the Vietnam War from fundamentally different perspectives. The Americans considered the conflict in Vietnam to be a part of a global ideological battle against communism. If Vietnam succeeded in establishing a communist state, they believed, communism would then spread to other nations in the region. The Vietnamese, by contrast, viewed the conflict as a civil war that was subject to the influence of outside interests.

This pattern of civil war and the struggle for independence from foreign control recurs throughout the long history of Vietnam. Vietnamese history goes back for thousands of years, but China dominated the land for a millennium. Later, the French imposed control on the nation during a critical period of growth, development, and suppression. The final invaders were the Americans, who involved themselves in the country's future soon after Vietnam freed itself from colonial rule.

Vietnam's landscape is dominated by its long coastline to the east and rugged mountain terrain to the west. Its neighbor to the north, China, influenced Vietnam's history for many centuries.

Vietnam's Origins

Vietnam's cultural identity dates back to the ancient, semi-mythical kingdom called Van Lang that was established in the Red River Valley about three thousand years ago. The settlers established a sophisticated culture based on rice farming and trade. Vietnam's recorded history begins in 208 BCE., when a Chinese warlord conquered the region and founded his own kingdom of Au Lac. Another invasion by a different Chinese faction led to the establishment of the kingdom of Nam Viet, which was annexed by China in 111 BCE.

China ruled Vietnam for the next millennium. China introduced technical innovations and profoundly influenced the culture and practices of Vietnam. But the Vietnamese people resented Chinese domination and never lost their sense of cultural identity. Nationalists staged occasional rebellions throughout China's long rule.

In 938, Vietnamese resistance defeated the Chinese in a naval battle. For most of its history after 939, Vietnam existed as an independent kingdom, although it expanded and split multiple times due to internal conflicts. The most dramatic division occurred in 1620, when the southern provinces split from the north and both halves maintained separate governments for more than one hundred years.

Meanwhile, Europeans had begun exploring and colonizing Asia. The Portuguese became the first Europeans to enter the region in 1535. France was especially intent on expanding its empire in Asia to include Vietnam, which was still involved in a civil war between the north and south. Independent of the French government, a French bishop provided ships, weapons, and fighters to an

Many of the people living in Vietnam's countryside are farmers who raise rice and other crops. Their way of life has not changed much over hundreds of years.

exiled prince from the southern ruling clan. The prince led a long rebellion that ultimately resulted in victory and reunification of Vietnam in 1802. He declared himself emperor Gia Long.

France's Colony

In 1856, Napoléon III, emperor of France, approved an invasion of Vietnam. Catholic missionaries in the region encouraged the conquest. Vietnam's rulers had resisted Catholic efforts to convert the Vietnamese people to Christianity. But France's motivations were primarily economic and political. Many of the other nations of Europe had established significant overseas territories in Africa, Asia, and the Americas. France looked to enhance its national prestige and exploit the potential economic opportunities of markets in Asia.[1]

French ships and troops arrived in 1858, easily occupying the port city of Tourane. In 1859, the fleet stormed Saigon. But Vietnamese resistance was fierce and the French were decimated by enemy assaults, unfamiliar tropical illnesses, and even the weather—they were unprepared for the monsoon rains.[2] Back in France, Napoléon III considered abandoning the attempt to subjugate Vietnam. Ultimately, though, France reinforced its military campaign and continued its push toward conquest. Little by little, the Vietnamese regime signed away territory through treaties and granted other concessions. But French ambitions for their colony went beyond plans for economic expansion. The invaders planned to impose French culture and institutions, as well.[3] After more than twenty years of fighting, the French seized the imperial capital of Hue and in 1883 officially established the protectorate that came to be known as French Indochina. Its borders would ultimately include present-day Cambodia and Laos, as well.

Under French control, the Vietnamese people were given only minor roles in government. Some of the Vietnamese elite collaborated with the French and grew wealthy, but most of the population of the subjugated nation struggled in dire poverty. The land and its resources were exploited for the benefit of France. Many farmers were displaced with the establishment of huge plantations growing crops such as rubber, coffee, and tea. Working conditions on the plantations and in the new mines and factories were often horrendous. Ordinary Vietnamese faced onerous tax burdens and saw their quality of life deteriorate.[4]

Fighting for Independence

French oppression sparked deep resentment against the colonial rulers. Several rebellions led by Vietnamese nationalists and guerrilla groups were attempted against French rule, but failed. Independence efforts strengthened after World War I, however, and groups of revolutionaries formed in opposition to the French. Intellectuals also began to publicly advocate reforms.

Nguyen Ai Quoc—better known as Ho Chi Minh—emerged as the leader of these efforts during the 1920s. Ho Chi Minh founded the Indochinese Communist Party in 1930. Vietnamese workers were devastated by the worldwide Great Depression, and Ho Chi Min's party staged a peasant uprising in 1931. The French brutally suppressed the uprising and Ho Chi Minh fled the country.

Ho Chi Minh was beloved by many Vietnamese people. He continued to wear peasant clothes even after becoming president of the Democratic Republic of Vietnam.

Ho Chi Minh in Paris

Born in 1890, Ho Chi Minh came from a highly educated family and studied at Vietnam's finest Franco-Vietnamese school. Ho's father was an ardent patriot, and Ho drew the attention of the authorities for his protest activities at a young age. In 1911, he departed Vietnam to wander the world. Ho took many odd jobs and lived for six years in France, where he became involved in left-wing politics. Later, he spent time in the Soviet Union, China, and other parts of Asia, and organized Vietnamese revolutionaries and communists with the support of the Soviets and Chinese. He did not return to Vietnam until 1941.

Ho was living in Paris in 1919 when the victorious Allies held the Paris Peace Conference, at which treaties were negotiated following the end of World War I. He drafted a petition calling for French government to end some of its oppressive practices toward its colonial subjects in Indochina and grant the native population more political and judicial rights and freedoms. The statement was distributed at the peace conference, but it received little notice from the official delegates. Ho's action did draw the favorable attention of French radicals, however, and his writings that were smuggled back into Vietnam made his name well known back at home.[5]

Vietnam was controlled by Japan for five years during World War II, from 1940 to 1945. During the course of the war, in 1941, Ho Chi Minh founded a group led by the Communist Party the called the Viet Minh, or "League for the Independence of Vietnam." With the Japanese surrender at the end of World War II, Ho Chi Minh led the Viet Minh in an uprising in August 1945. The group seized control of Hanoi in the north and Ho Chi Minh declared the nation's independence, creating the Democratic Republic of Vietnam.

France continued to maintain a presence in southern Vietnam and hoped to regain control of it colonies. In 1946, France negotiated with the Democratic Republic of Vietnam to develop a plan under which the two regimes could coexist peacefully. Late in the year however, talks broke down and the French bombed the port city of Haiphong. The Viet Minh struck back in December and General Vo Nguyen Giap called for a national uprising against the French. These events marked the beginning of the First Indochina War. In 1949, the Viet Minh gained the military backing of communist China. The Cold War—the ideological conflict between communist states and the democratic West—was beginning to take root. Although intelligence operatives working for the United States had cooperated with Ho Chi Minh during World War II, the United States chose to support France in the conflict. The United States viewed the war as one element of the larger struggle against communism.

The war dragged on for eight years, leaving 400 thousand soldiers and civilians dead.[6] After suffering a crippling defeat at the Battle of Dien Bien Phu in 1954, France negotiated a cease-fire known as the Geneva Accords. The agreement split Vietnam into halves along the 17th parallel marking northern latitude. The communist Democratic Republic of Vietnam was established in the north, headquartered at Hanoi, and the Republic of Vietnam in the south, based in Saigon. However, it called for the nation to be unified by elections within a few years.

> **"The whole Vietnamese people, animated by a common purpose, are determined to fight to the bitter end against any attempt by the French colonists to reconquer their country.**
>
> **We are convinced that the Allied nations which at Tehran and San Francisco have acknowledged the principles of self-determination and equality of nations, will not refuse to acknowledge the independence of Vietnam."**
>
> —*Ho Chi Minh, the Vietnamese Declaration of Independence, 1945*[7]

A Fragile Peace

France departed Vietnam in 1956, leaving behind a devastated land with an uncertain future. Soon after the agreement was signed, nearly a million Vietnamese had fled from the north to the south.[8] Neither side adhered to the terms of the Geneva Accords. The United States quickly moved to channel money and military advisors to the Saigon government. The CIA took part in sabotage and propaganda efforts against the North Vietnamese.

Ho Chi Minh—referred to as "Uncle Ho"—was popular throughout Vietnam as a heroic patriot. Ho purged his enemies in North Vietnam and divided private lands into small farms.

In the south, the anticommunist leader Ngo Dinh Diem was named Prime Minister in 1955, supported by

South Vietnam's president Ngo Dinh Diem came from a noble family and had been a government official during the French colonial years. He was a dedicated foe of communism.

the Americans. Unlike Ho, he was unable to command the loyalty of the Vietnamese. He was seen as distant, arrogant, and repressive. Under his command, secret police executed and jailed people who had fought against France or sympathized with Ho Chi Minh. His government was corrupt and undemocratic. The nationwide reunification elections were postponed, largely because Diem and the Americans believed that Ho Chi Minh would prevail.

Ho Chi Minh still fervently hoped for the reunification of Vietnam, even after the 1956 deadline for elections passed by. As resistance to Diem's regime strengthened in the south, fighters that came to be known as Viet Cong began launching guerrilla attacks against the government. To the north, the communist regime began building the Ho Chi Minh Trail in 1959. This network of jungle routes allowed the North Vietnamese to transport fighters, supplies, and weapons into South Vietnam.

In July of 1959, guerrilla fighters opened fire in the small town of Bien Hoa, the site of a South Vietnamese army base. Among the dead were Major Dale Buis and Master Sergeant Chester Ovnand, two military advisors sent by the United States—and the first Americans killed in the conflict that became known as the Vietnam War.[9]

ESCALATION IN ASIA

Lyndon Johnson's Senate career progressed smoothly, even as the US became increasingly involved in the conflict in Vietnam. When fighting broke out between North Vietnam and South Vietnam in 1959, the fighting seemed distant to many people in the United States.

The presidential campaign of 1960 attracted more media attention than the war in Vietnam. Despite his strong leadership record in the Senate, Johnson was passed over for the Democratic presidential nomination in 1960. Johnson had decided to skip the state primaries and try to win the nomination at the Democratic National Convention, when delegates from each state would cast votes for the candidate they thought would be the best candidate. There were twelve other candidates vying for the nomination at the convention.

Johnson finished second in the delegate voting, behind Massachusetts senator John F. Kennedy. The dynamic Kennedy had won commanding victories in several primaries before the convention. Like Johnson, Kennedy was a shrewd politician. He belonged to the Roman Catholic faith at a time when Catholics still faced discrimination in some parts of the country. He was also from the north and had spoken in favor of civil rights legislation, making it hard for him to win support from southern voters. Kennedy chose Johnson to serve as his running mate. That November, Kennedy and Johnson ended up winning a very close election against Vice President Richard M. Nixon. Suddenly, Lyndon Johnson was the second most powerful man in the United States.

Deeper Involvement

When Kennedy and Johnson took office in 1961, they inherited the growing US role in Vietnam from the Eisenhower administration. The US had sent money and military advisors to support the government in South Vietnam. However, Eisenhower had been reluctant to commit fighting soldiers to the war, despite pressure from some members of Congress to use military force in preventing the spread of communism. There were fewer than 800 military personnel in Vietnam when Kennedy took office.

The war in Vietnam had not been a major factor in the 1960 election, though Kennedy viewed the spread of communism as a threat to democracy. Tensions with the Soviet Union were extremely high, especially after a secret operation by the Central Intelligence Agency (CIA) against Soviet-backed Cuba—later known as the Bay of Pigs invasion—failed in April 1961, just a few weeks into Kennedy's administration.

President John F. Kennedy took office when US efforts to support the South Vietnamese government were failing. However, he believed that it would be a mistake to withdraw from Vietnam.

He and Johnson, along with the presidential cabinet, crafted a flexible policy toward defending against the Soviet Union that would give the US many options in countering communism. This included sending more military advisers into South Vietnam in an effort to help South Vietnamese forces fight against North Vietnam. China, North Korea, and Laos were all communist nations and influenced by the Soviet Union. Kennedy did not want the Soviet Union to gain the same influence over South Vietnam. In fact, he sent Johnson to the South Vietnamese capital in Saigon to reinforce the US commitment to South Vietnam.

The Domino Theory

The Domino Theory was the Cold War–era notion that a communist government in one nation would influence neighboring countries to become communist. The idea was first spelled out by President Dwight Eisenhower during a press conference given in April of 1954, when the United States was providing aid to the French as they tried to hold on to Vietnam. "You have a row of dominoes set up, you knock over the first one, and what will happen to the last one is a certainty that it will go over very quickly," Eisenhower told reporters. Eventually, all of Southeast Asia would fall. Both Kennedy and Johnson would go on to use the Domino Theory to justify their efforts to keep South Vietnam out of the hands of communists.[1]

Throughout his presidency, Kennedy continued to increase the number of soldiers and money sent over to South Vietnam. In 1962, the number of US military personnel in South Vietnam had climbed to nearly nine thousand.

The US military had become more active in the conflict, as well. In January 1962, the US Army began a joint operation with the Army of the Republic of Vietnam. "Operation Chopper," as it was called, involved using US Army helicopters to transport South Vietnamese paratroopers in a surprise attack against a North Vietnamese base near Saigon. The attack was a success and marked the first direct involvement of US troops in the conflict. [2]

The US and South Vietnamese forces had major technological advantages over North Vietnam. The helicopters were still fairly new technology. Many Viet Cong fighters had never seen them before and had no idea how to fight against them. In time, however, they would learn to adapt.

Diem's Fall

The weapons, funding, and military training that the US provided to South Vietnam helped slow the Viet Cong forces, which continued to follow the Ho Chi Minh Trail southward. However, even with support from US helicopters, South Vietnamese forces continued to fare poorly against the Viet Cong. Intense guerrilla warfare continued between the two sides. In fact, many of the people living in South Vietnam were still loyal to North Vietnamese leader Ho Chi Minh due to his leadership during the struggle for independence from France. Many were also sympathetic to North Vietnam. They wanted their country to be united instead of split between the communist north and the south, led by the autocratic government of President Ngo Dinh Diem. Some helped the Viet Cong fighters, or even joined them.

Diem himself was a major cause of these defections. Under his leadership, the government of South Vietnam was hopelessly corrupt and ineffective. He had wiped out democratic reforms and put many of his own relatives in positions of power. His efforts to fight against the pro-communist forces were ineffective and relied heavily on bringing in funds and weapons from the United States.

Diem was also a Roman Catholic in a nation in which Buddhism was the most widespread religion. Diem showed strong favoritism toward other Catholics, heightening his unpopularity among the Buddhist majority. He failed to follow through on land reforms that he had promised when he became president, and he and his family used their government positions to make themselves rich.[3]

People who opposed Diem's policies and tactics were often put in prison and were accused of helping the communist fighters. Many were killed. When Buddhists began holding protests against Diem in 1963, the government reacted with force in what became known as the Buddhist Crisis. Buddhists were not allowed to gather or fly the Buddhist flag during celebrations of the Buddha's birthday that May. South Vietnamese soldiers even shot into crowds during a protest in the city of Hue, killing several people. Diem's brother and close advisor Ngo Dinh Nhu was suspected of being the real source of the heavy-handed policies against the Buddhists. The demonstrations continued through the summer, coming to a head in June when a Buddhist monk publicly set himself on fire and burned to death as an act of protest.

President Kennedy was growing more reluctant to support Diem's government. That summer, he tried to convince Diem to carry out government reforms that might help unify South Vietnam. Instead, President Diem ignored Kennedy and declared martial law in Saigon. His supporters closed Buddhist monasteries and made more arrests.

The protests and actions of Diem's government had put the US in a difficult position. President Kennedy believed that US forces needed to stay in South Vietnam. Diem's unpopularity and unwillingness to carry out reforms made it very difficult to do so. Kennedy even sent US Ambassador Henry Cabot Lodge to South Vietnam to find out whether there was a way to peacefully remove Diem from power and replace his government. Lodge reported back that Diem was unlikely to leave office unless he was forced out in a coup. South Vietnamese military leaders even approached Lodge with the idea of staging a military takeover with support from the US

Many of South Vietnam's military leaders were unhappy with Diem's treatment of Buddhists and his strategies against the North Vietnamese invaders. Like many people in South Vietnam, they wanted to end the fighting with the North. The Kennedy administration did not want to be directly involved in a coup, but sent a telegram to Lodge. The message, which came to be known as Cable 243, instructed Lodge to take no action in the event that the South Vietnamese military staged a coup.[4]

The coup that the US had been expecting came on November 1, 1963. A general named Duong Van Minh led the coup, which went fairly smoothly. In Saigon,

South Vietnamese soldiers took control of radio stations and the police headquarters, while tanks surrounded the presidential palace. Many of the government officials who were loyal to Diem were captured easily and without a fight. Diem and Nhu, however, were aware that plans were being made for a coup and had made arrangements to escape. They were cornered in Saigon and convinced to surrender. They gave themselves up on November 2, 1963. Minh and the other generals who led the coup had intended to send the brothers into exile. Instead, they

A South Vietnamese soldier taking part in the military coup against President Ngo Dinh Diem stands in the presidential palace shortly after its capture. Diem had fled the building.

attempted to escape and were quickly recaptured. Their captors then murdered them.[5]

The Darkest Day

More chaos followed the military's coup against Diem's government and his execution. President Kennedy was shocked by the execution of Diem and his brother Nhu. Ambassador Lodge, however, sent Kennedy a message to reassure him that the removal of Diem and his brother would likely hasten the end of the conflict.

President Kennedy himself had very little time to consider how the coup and assassinations would affect US policies in Vietnam. On November 22, 1963, Kennedy was shot to death while riding in a motorcade in downtown Dallas, Texas. Texas Governor John Connelly, who was riding beside Kennedy, was also shot and seriously wounded. Kennedy was pronounced dead upon his arrival at Dallas's Parkland Hospital. Lyndon Johnson was also riding in the motorcade, though he was not in the same car as Kennedy.

Johnson was deeply shaken by the president's murder, but he was resolved to fulfill his duties as vice president. This meant that he would have to become president. Shortly after Kennedy was pronounced dead, his body was loaded onto Air Force One, accompanied by Johnson and Kennedy's wife, First Lady Jacqueline Kennedy. On the plane, Federal Judge Sarah T. Hughes administered the Oath of Office to Johnson with Jacqueline Kennedy at his side. The United States suddenly had a new president.[6]

Kennedy had agonized over what to do about Vietnam. The military coup in South Vietnam and the assassination

Hours after Kennedy's assassination, Johnson is sworn in as president of the United States onboard Air Force One. Jacqueline Kennedy stands by his side.

of Diem had made the way forward even less clear for the US, despite Lodge's belief that the war would wind down more quickly without Diem's family in power. After he was sworn in and had returned to Washington, DC, Johnson promised to follow Kennedy's policies in Vietnam. He told Lodge that he would not lose Vietnam.

Setting an Agenda

Johnson had finally risen to the presidency, but in the saddest way possible. The United States remained deep in mourning for President Kennedy and his unrealized potential. Kennedy had successfully handled foreign crises before. He had brought the United States back from the brink of nuclear war in 1962, when the Soviet Union had moved nuclear missiles onto a base in Cuba, within striking distance of the US

Johnson was less experienced in foreign affairs. He was much more confident in his ability to set a progressive agenda at home. Early in his administration, he set out ambitious goals that reflected back on his years as a New Deal Democrat in Congress and his early years in Texas. They also advanced many of President Kennedy's plans. Johnson felt that he should honor Kennedy's intentions by working to make his vision for the future a reality.[7]

Johnson laid out many of his plans in his first State of the Union address, delivered to Congress on January 8, 1964. In the speech, he laid out his plans for passing stronger civil rights laws and for helping people overcome poverty, as well as ideas for providing senior citizens with medical care. He declared an all-out "war on poverty."

"Poverty is a national problem, requiring improved national organization and support. But this attack, to be effective, must also be organized at the State and the local level and must be supported and directed by State and local efforts. For the war against poverty will not be won here in Washington. It must be won in the field, in every private home, in every public office, from the courthouse to the White House."[8]

—Lyndon Johnson, first State of the Union Address, January 8, 1964

The War on Poverty sought to lift people out of poverty with social programs that were designed to provide economic aid to the United States' poorest citizens. This included providing help with medical care, early education, unemployment assistance, and covering basic needs such as food. Medicaid, Food Stamps, and the Head Start early education program all grew out of this strategy.

Johnson's address also touched on his plans for guaranteeing equality under the law to all citizens, regardless of race, through passage of stronger civil rights laws. Unlike the earlier law, Johnson's new civil rights laws would include strong enforcement measures. He argued that all members of the public should have equal access to good public schools, facilities, and the right to vote.[9]

ASSESSING VIETNAM

Johnson was very conscious of how history would view US involvement in Vietnam. He was the fourth president to have to deal with the conflict, and the US was more deeply involved than ever when he took office. He did not want to be seen as the president who had lost the conflict, even though US forces were not yet directly involved in the fighting. This reluctance to lose would come to dominate his policies in Vietnam.

The Weight of History

US involvement in Vietnam had increased during Kennedy's presidency, but Kennedy himself was reluctant to commit ground troops to help South Vietnam fight off Viet Cong forces. Instead, the US continued to send money and military advisers. Kennedy was shocked by Diem's assassination, but left no sign of his intentions before his own murder.

Becoming president had satisfied Johnson's ultimate ambition, and it gave him the opportunity to follow through with the social programs and civil rights measures that were close to his heart. He likely expected to navigate a tangled relationship with the Soviet Union, as presidents Dwight Eisenhower and John F. Kennedy had before him. It probably never crossed his mind that Vietnam would become the foreign policy issue that would define his presidency.

Johnson had inherited a growing conflict that had only grown more complicated. By the end of 1963, the US had about 16,300 military advisors in Vietnam and was spending millions of dollars to keep South Vietnam's army together.[1] Despite the spending and the presence of US troops who were supposed to train the South Vietnamese army, the war was going very badly for South Vietnam. Much of South Vietnam's countryside was controlled by

North Vietnamese soldiers place explosive mines on the beach near the city of Dong Hoi. Such traps made it extremely difficult for soldiers to move safely through the countryside.

Viet Cong fighters. Only the areas around Saigon were secure. The US Army had little faith that South Vietnamese forces would be able to hold off the Viet Cong for much longer.

The dynamics of the Cold War with the Soviet Union put a great deal of pressure on Johnson. Much of Southeast Asia was viewed as a point of conflict between the US and the Soviet Union. During the 1950s, the US had managed to keep North Korean communists that were supported by The Soviet Union and China from overrunning South Korea. Johnson was determined to prevent Vietnam from reunifying under a communist government. When he first took office, he also shared Kennedy's reluctance to commit large numbers of fighting forces to the war. Much of his handling of the war would be marked by this ambivalence.[2]

Developing Strategies

Conditions in South Vietnam steadily grew worse through early 1964. The Viet Cong controlled about 40 percent of the countryside. Things had also not stabilized politically following Diem's removal and assassination. The generals who had taken control of the government were not able to govern well. A series of civilian leaders and military governments followed, with none of them able to bring the country under control.[3]

Johnson had kept many of Kennedy's close advisors in their positions. He wanted to follow Kennedy's intentions as closely as possible. One of the most important members of his cabinet to carry over from Kennedy's administration was Secretary of Defense Robert McNamara. McNamara, a former automotive executive, was known for being thoughtful and driven. He had been appointed to his position at the beginning of Kennedy's term and had overseen the escalation US involvement in Vietnam. An analysis of the conflict that McNamara carried out in 1962 indicated that the US could successfully wrap up its operations there within four years.[4]

Johnson relied heavily on McNamara to bring US involvement in Vietnam to a successful conclusion and believed in his analysis. In March of 1964 he sent McNamara to South Vietnam as a show of support for Khanh. McNamara pledged that the United States would provide whatever aid would be necessary and would stay in South Vietnam for as long as it would take to defeat the communist fighters swarming throughout the country. "We are here to emphasize that the United States will maintain its interest and its presence in your country," McNamara said during his speech. "There is no question whatsoever of our abandoning that interest."[5]

The North Vietnamese intensified their attacks in South Vietnam's countryside and prepared for a long war. The Viet Cong fighters did not have the advanced weaponry and technology of the US They relied on stealth and knowledge of the countryside to pull off their attacks. For the most part, they had to travel by foot over rugged terrain, often dragging their equipment behind them in order to get to where they were going. The Viet Cong made improvements along the Ho Chi Minh Trail to make it easier to move soldiers and equipment. The trail became capable of handling large vehicles and heavy equipment. They built a massive network of tunnels, bunkers, and traps through the mountains and jungles. These networks were well-stocked

Members of the US Army Special Forces (Green Berets) train South Vietnamese soldiers in marksmanship. The US worked hard to help modernize South Vietnam's army.

"We are very anxious to do what we can to help those people preserve their own freedom. We cherish ours and we would like to see them preserve theirs. We have furnished them with counsel and advice, and men and material to help them in their attempts to defend themselves. If people would quit attacking them we'd have no problem, but for 10 years this problem has been going on."[6]

—Lyndon Johnson, speaking during a March 15, 1964, press conference

with weapons, food, medical supplies, and other necessities. They would eventually provide a key defense against attacks from the air.[7]

Hearts and Minds

Besides reassuring South Vietnam's government that the US would continue to provide support, Johnson's early efforts in 1964 revolved around winning over the population of South Vietnam. The US began several programs designed to accomplish this goal.

Many of Diem's efforts to combat North Vietnam invaders and the people in South Vietnam who helped them were violent and heavy-handed. These included widespread arrests and executions of people suspected of being sympathetic to the Viet Cong.

In 1962, Diem's government and the US worked together on a project called the Strategic Hamlet Program. The program was designed to separate people living in the countryside from possible North Vietnamese influences. South Vietnam used US funds and advice to build protected villages, or "hamlets," where South Vietnam's government would be able to help them with food and defense. The government would also be able to use the villages to isolate communists through regular identification checks.

The US had hoped that rural people would move into the hamlets on their own, but few did so. Diem's government forced people to relocate into the hamlets. Instead of building closer ties between the government and the rural population, the program isolated the people in the countryside and drove many to join the fighting against the government.[8] Many of the hamlets were destroyed after Diem's death.

Johnson sought to reverse these losses. He sent more funds to South Vietnam and started a major propaganda campaign against North Vietnam. He also sent people with professional skills to help with programs designed to win the hearts and minds of people in South Vietnam. These included teachers, doctors, and farmers. Johnson believed that the people could be won over with better health care, education, and by learning new farming methods. He also started infrastructure programs, including new hospitals, roads, and schools. These efforts turned out to be less successful than he had hoped.[9]

Controlling the Senate

Before becoming vice president, Johnson had been a very successful leader in the Senate. He mastered the art of arguing, persuading, and sometimes even bullying other senators to vote for legislation he thought was important. After taking the leading role in passing civil rights legislation in 1958, he also became an important bridge between older, more conservative Democrats and their younger, more liberal counterparts. He could also communicate equally effectively with the anti-integration southern Democrats and progressive northerners who wanted to end racist government policies.

Typically, it is the vice president's job to lead the Senate. Vice presidents are responsible for presiding over the Senate. They don't introduce legislation, but they can use their influence to convince senators to vote one way or another. They can also make recommendations on how

The Great Society

Johnson's ambitious domestic agenda was in full swing in 1964, even as the situation in Vietnam was growing more complicated. He called the vision that he had for the United States "The Great Society." It was a vision of upward mobility in which the federal government would provide the tools people needed to elevate themselves out of poverty and end discrimination. The idea included the rebuilding of American cities with modern housing and reliable public transportation and efforts to eliminate pollution from the air and water. A good education for everyone through federally funded schools rounded out his vision, some of which he had outlined in his State of the Union address. He formally introduced the idea of The Great Society in a speech at the University of Michigan in Ann Arbor in May of 1964, which was met with enthusiastic applause.

legislation should be written and can vote in the event of a tie. Johnson did not have a vice president when he first took office—the US Constitution was not amended to permit a president to appoint a vice president until 1967. Even without a vice president, Johnson still had a lot of influence in Congress.[10]

The House of Representatives and the Senate were both dividing into two sides on the issue of Vietnam and how the growing conflict should be treated. Those who wanted the US to begin direct military operations were called "hawks," for the bird of prey. They wanted the US to start a large-scale bombing campaign in North Vietnam. They also believed that threatening to invade North Vietnam would convince Ho Chi Minh's government to end its efforts in South Vietnam. Some hawks also pushed for more than 1 million US troops to be sent to Vietnam in order to block North Vietnam from crossing over into South Vietnam to assist the Viet

Other people in Congress wanted to bring the conflict to a peaceful end. They were called "doves," after the bird that is commonly recognized as a symbol of peace. The doves were opposed to sending any more military aid to South Vietnam. Many wanted US involvement in Vietnam to end completely. Johnson had to keep both sides talking and cooperating if he wanted to accomplish any of his goals, such as passage of civil rights legislation. While he pursued peaceful efforts to win over people in South Vietnam, he also committed another four thousand military personnel to South Vietnam.[11]

THE MIDDLE COURSE

Johnson attempted to steer a path between those who wanted to increase involvement in the Vietnam conflict and those who wanted to end all military activity in the nation. He did not want the US to be caught up in a long and bloody war overseas. The US had fought in the Korean War (1950–1953) on the behalf of South Korea against communist North Korea just over a decade before. North Korea was supported by the Soviet Union and China, and the US government saw that war as a struggle to keep communism from spreading throughout Asia. While the US succeeded in keeping North Korea from taking control of South Korea, the fighting had been intense and casualties were high. The US lost approximately 36,900 military personnel during that relatively short war.[1] The Korean War essentially ended in a draw and resulted in Korea being two divided nations.

Johnson wanted to find a way out of Vietnam, but he was under intense pressure to keep South Vietnam out of communist hands. The conflict was also a key factor in the upcoming presidential election. Johnson would have to prove to the people of the United States that he was tough enough to not back down against the communist threat. He would also have to show that he was shrewd enough to keep the US commitment as minimal as possible.

Peace Platform

Johnson was very popular at the beginning of his presidency. The nation was still grieving over Kennedy's assassination, and Johnson had promised to stick to Kennedy's agenda as he finished out the term. Johnson's approval rating for the first six months of his presidency was at or above 75 percent, meaning that a large majority of Americans believed that he was doing a good job.[2] However, he still considered himself to be filling in for Kennedy and was unsure of whether he could win a presidential election on his own. He had not done well in the 1960 Democratic primaries, after all.

Johnson's stance on civil rights and fighting poverty, as well as his promises to cut taxes also helped keep his popularity ratings up. He could also point to his record in the Senate as evidence that he could accomplish his goals. There was little doubt that Johnson would become the Democratic Party's nominee, though Kennedy's brother, US Attorney General Robert Kennedy, was considered a strong alternate candidate. Many people wanted Johnson to choose Kennedy as his running mate, though the two men did not get along well. Johnson also faced some opposition from segregationist Democrats in the south, who supported Alabama governor George Wallace.

In the end, Johnson won the nomination easily. In addition to his civil rights and anti-poverty platform, he

Lyndon Johnson greets supporters while campaigning in the months before the 1964 presidential election. At that time, Johnson's policies toward Vietnam enjoyed widespread support.

also ran on the promise to end the Vietnam conflict in a way that would be favorable to the US Johnson positioned himself as a candidate who would work for global peace. Throughout the campaign, he promised to work with other nations to bring about lasting peace and to avoid nuclear warfare, which was a very real threat in 1964. When talking about Vietnam and the possibility of increasing US involvement, he said that the US was "not about to send American boys nine or ten thousand miles from home to do what Asian boys ought to be doing for themselves."[3]

"We are going to continue to try to make these people more effective and more efficient, and do our best to resolve that situation where the aggressors will leave their neighbors alone, and they will finally learn to live together in peace as they have in other parts of the world. So we are going to assist them against attack as we have. We will work to help them achieve progress and self-confidence. We will not permit the independent nations of the East to be swallowed up by communist conquest."

—Lyndon Johnson, during a campaign speech at Akron University, October 21, 1964[4]

The Gulf of Tonkin Incident

Despite Johnson's interest in finding a way out of Vietnam, the conflict continued to heat up. On August 2 and August 4, 1964, the US Navy destroyers USS *Maddox* and USS *C. Turner Joy* were reportedly attacked by North Vietnamese ships in the Gulf of Tonkin, which is located off the coast of North Vietnam in the South China Sea. In both incidents, the warships were fired on without cause by North Vietnamese torpedo boats. The ships were in international waters at the time, meaning that North Vietnam had no just cause to fire at them.

South Vietnam had been carrying out secret attacks against North Vietnam from the gulf since early 1964. The US had provided support for these operations. Under the leadership of Lieutenant General Wesley C. Westmoreland, who led the US Military Assistance Command, those operations intensified into full-scale coastal bombardments of radar facilities. South Vietnamese boats fired rifles, mortars, and rockets at North Vietnamese positions. The two ships had been gathering information that could be useful in these missions.[5]

Decades later, declassified documents released by the US National Security Agency showed that the USS *Maddox* was definitely attacked on August 2, and that the incident had happened after a South Vietnamese attack on the coastline. The US Navy had intercepted messages that appeared to show that North Vietnam planned to attack the *Maddox*. When the ship's commander saw the three gunboats approaching at a high rate of speed, he ordered his crew to fire if the ships came within a certain distance. The *Maddox* had fired first on the North Vietnamese boats, shooting over the front of the first North Vietnamese ship as a warning. The North Vietnamese ships returned fire and launched torpedoes. When the shooting was over, the *Maddox* and US Navy planes destroyed one of the North Vietnamese ships and heavily damaged the other two.

The facts were further twisted regarding the supposed attack on the USS *C. Turner Joy*. The *Maddox* had been undamaged in the exchange of fire and was back in the gulf on August 4. Johnson also ordered the *Turner Joy* into the gulf as a show of US strength. The night before, South Vietnamese forces had again carried out an attack against a North Vietnamese facility. The *Turner Joy* and the *Maddox* were more than 100 miles away from the coast of North Vietnam and sailing in low visibility conditions when the

Maddox reported unidentified ships appearing on its sonar equipment. The ships appeared to come from all directions, and the *Maddox* reported numerous attacks as the enemy targets kept disappearing and reappearing. Both ships spent several hours going through maneuvers to evade the attacking ships, and the *Maddox* fired hundreds of shells.[6]

The attacks on US ships immediately drew the US deeper into the war. The military had avoided direct fighting with the North Vietnamese, but these incidents broke the pattern.

Many years later, the unclassified NSA documents showed that the August 4 attack likely never happened at all. The *Maddox*'s commander, Captain John Herrick, decided that his crew had probably been overeager and the ship's sonar was malfunctioning, resulting in the crew "seeing" ships and torpedoes in the water that weren't actually there.

There was a great deal of confusion in Washington, DC, regarding the August 4 attack. Herrick believed that there had been an attack at the beginning and that torpedoes had passed near the *Maddox*, though no one actually saw any torpedoes. His commander, Admiral US Grant Sharp, believed there was a possibility that the attack on the *Maddox* never happened and informed Secretary of Defense McNamara of this belief. McNamara consulted with US intelligence agencies, who said that an attack probably had occurred.[7]

McNamara decided the attack probably did take place and informed Johnson. Later that night, Johnson went on television to talk about the attack and to announce his intention to launch a US attack in retaliation. Just a few hours later, US aircraft began bombing North Vietnamese coastal facilities, including a fuel depot and four naval bases. The oil depot and several North Vietnamese ships were destroyed.[8]

Congressional Resolution

Johnson had said many times that he did not want to involve the US in a drawn-out war or commit more military personnel to South Vietnam, but the Gulf of Tonkin Incident changed that. He was committed to working on his War on Poverty and civil rights issues at home and had no desire to commit soldiers and more money to the conflict in Vietnam. However, he also worried that the US would lose some of its standing as a dominant global superpower if he pulled US personnel out.

The attacks—both the real one and the one is now widely acknowledged to have been imagined—raised tensions in Vietnam and within the US government to new levels. There was a great deal of support for striking back hard against North Vietnam.

On August 5, 1964, Johnson approached Congress to ask for permission to take military action in Vietnam. By that time, he knew that the first attack had been provoked and that the second attack had likely never happened. Nonetheless, he wanted to have the power to respond to threats to the stability of the nations in Southeast Asia as they emerged and to send in fighting forces if necessary. This included not only South Vietnam but also Cambodia, Laos, Thailand, and other nations in the region in the event that the conflict spread. Essentially, Johnson was asking for the power to fight a war without actually declaring war against North Vietnam. He was abandoning his carefully plotted middle road.[9]

Many members of Congress were eager to strike back hard against North Vietnam. For the moment, the hawks were the dominant voice. They put enormous pressure on Johnson to expand the US military role. Johnson was still reluctant to start a war during a year in which he was up for reelection. On the side of the doves, some members of Congress had heard rumors that the US Navy provoked the attack by assisting in South Vietnam's attacks. They wanted to get out of Vietnam completely. Johnson's administration let the hawks know that the US had probably provoked the attacks and that large-scale retaliation was not yet necessary. He and his cabinet continued to tell the public that the attacks had been unprovoked.

On August 7, 1964, Congress passed the bill that Johnson wanted. Called the Gulf of Tonkin Resolution, it gave Johnson vast powers to carry out a full-scale war in Southeast Asia.

There was very little debate on the issue in Congress. The House of Representatives passed the resolution unanimously—voting 416–0—after only forty minutes of debate. The senate debated for nine hours, but in the end voted 88–2 to approve the legislation. Only two senators opposed it—Ernest Gruening of Alaska and Wayne Morse of Oregon. Both were Democrats.[10]

Johnson was happy with the resolution. It gave him vast powers to fight the war as he and his cabinet saw fit. They would be able to act decisively against the North Vietnamese without having to navigate between the hawks and the doves in Congress.

Decisive Reelection

Johnson's reelection campaign ran very smoothly throughout the spring and summer of 1964. His popularity had been very high since he took office. His handling of the Gulf of Tonkin Incident allowed him to appear calm and in control, while also showing that he was willing to take action when US interests were at stake. His approval ratings rose immediately after passage of the Gulf of Tonkin Resolution.

Johnson's domestic policies also made him popular. He wanted to develop domestic policies that echoed the New Deal reforms of Franklin Roosevelt, in which government was given a much bigger role in the lives of individuals. While campaigning, he continued to talk about the "War on Poverty" and expanding the federal government to create a "Great Society" in which every American would have equal opportunities. The Civil Rights Act of 1964, which he had signed into law on July 2, provided protection against discrimination based on a person's race, color, religion or country of origin. It also established the groundwork for federal education funding and other programs that were part of the War on Poverty.

Early on in the campaign, Johnson had been pressured to pick the popular Attorney General Robert Kennedy as his vice presidential running mate. Instead, he chose Senator Hubert H. Humphrey of Minnesota to balance the ticket. Humphrey was from a northern state and was more liberal in his politics than Johnson. Johnson believed that Humphrey's presence as his running mate would help bring in more voters. Johnson also expected to lose some of the "Solid South" states to his opponents, including Segregationist George Wallace's racist campaign.

The Republican Party nominee was Senator Barry Goldwater of Arizona. Goldwater was the opposite of Johnson in many ways and was strongly opposed to government spending of any kind. He was also very anti-communist and saw the War on Poverty programs Johnson proposed as a form of socialism. Goldwater had actually voted against the Civil Rights Act and spend much of his time on the campaign trail talking about urban crime. His campaign made little effort to attract African American voters, who flocked to Johnson.[11]

Johnson waged a very negative campaign against Goldwater. The campaign painted Goldwater as extremely conservative and pro-war, a position that was exploited in the famous "Daisy Ad." Goldwater's vote against the Civil Rights Act and calls to cut popular social programs such as Social Security led many moderate Republicans to either vote against him or not vote at all. Johnson won the election in a landslide on November 3, winning by more than 15 million votes.

Committing to Vietnam

Even before his big win in the presidential election, military leaders were pushing to convince Johnson to send soldiers to Vietnam. He resisted calls to carry out another major air strike when Viet Cong soldiers launched a mortar attack against US troops in November, killing five US soldiers and two South Vietnamese fighters, while wounding nearly one hundred others. A bombing by Viet Cong terrorists that killed two US Army officers in December was also ignored.

The buildup of troops continued. By the end of 1964, there were twenty-three thousand US troops in South

The Daisy Ad

Johnson's "Daisy ad" shows a little girl plucking petals off of a daisy, the scene broken into by a man's voice counting down from ten to one. Then footage of a nuclear explosion and mushroom cloud appears as Johnson himself says, "These are the stakes—to make a world in which all of God's children can live, or to go into the dark. We must either love each other, or we must die."[12]

The Daisy ad was only shown once on television, on September 7, 1964. Unlike campaign ads typical of the time, it appealed to the viewer's emotions rather than by using facts to make the case. The Daisy ad didn't even mention Johnson's opponent by name. Instead, it implied with images that Goldwater could not be trusted with the nation's nuclear arsenal.

Public response to the Daisy ad was instantaneous. After it aired, the White House phone lines were swamped with calls protesting the ad. Goldwater referred to it as "weird television advertising" that insulted Americans' intelligence. Nonetheless, the Daisy ad is now considered the most famous political ad in history, and it had a critical long-term impact on the way political candidates used attack ads.[13]

Vietnam. Johnson's top military advisors, McNamara and National Security Advisor McGeorge Bundy, were recommending a steady buildup of soldiers who could strike against the estimated 170,000 North Vietnamese and Viet Cong fighters that formed what Ho Chi Minh called the People's Revolutionary Army in South Vietnam.

Early in 1965, McNamara and Bundy again pushed for more troops to be sent to Vietnam because the strategy of limited American involvement was failing. They told Johnson that the US was coming to a "fork in the road" and that he would soon have to either commit more soldiers or end American involvement.

Johnson finally did so in February of 1965, first ordering a bombing campaign against a North Vietnamese army camp after a US command post was attacked by Viet Cong fighters in the city of Pleiku. He did so without making any announcement to the public. Few Americans realized it at the time, but the Vietnam War had begun in earnest.[14]

SHIFTING MOMENTUM

The air strike against North Vietnam—code named Operation Flaming Dart—was only the beginning of America's display of military might. Though the American public did not learn about the bombing until afterward, public support was strong for the attack and for Johnson. A few weeks later, General Westmoreland requested that Johnson send him US Marines to defend against a possible North Vietnamese attack against a US air base at Da Nang. Johnson sent the requested troops The two battalions of marines—about 3,500 soldiers—landed on the beach in full combat gear and with their guns ready on March 8, 1965. The land war was about to begin.

The US ambassador in South Vietnam, Maxwell Taylor, objected to the military buildup. Taylor warned the president that America was on the verge of making the same mistakes the French colonists had. France had kept committing soldiers to their own war in Vietnam, only to lose. Johnson and his advisors, particularly McNamara, understood that the ongoing political instability and the actions of Viet Cong guerrillas were leading South Vietnam close to collapse. They believed that the only way to keep the country out of the hands of the communists was to increase the US military presence.[1]

Early Successes

Johnson and his advisors were optimistic that American firepower could beat North Vietnam. They also assumed that the size of the US military would overpower North Vietnam's army. In 1964 and 1965, the US military had more than 2.6 million personnel spread out across the Army, the Navy, the Air Force and the Marine Corps.[2]

Paratroopers from the US Army's 173rd Airborne Division patrol the countryside. The US military used some of its most versatile soldiers to try to match the Viet Cong guerrillas.

These numbers were bolstered by the Selective Service's peacetime draft lottery. US law requires men between the ages of eighteen and twenty-six to register with the Selective Service. They get a number, and if a draft is held and their number is called, they have to join the military for a certain length of time. Usually, the draft was held only in times of war, but the US held a draft nearly every year since 1940, even when the nation was not fighting. In 1964, 112,386 men were drafted to serve in the military. That number would more than double in 1965, when nearly 231,000 men were drafted. With a strong volunteer military and millions of potential draftees, the US had the biggest military in the world.[3]

Once he started sending troops, Johnson continued to build up their numbers. More than 184,000 American soldiers were stationed in Vietnam by the end of 1965. At the war's peak in 1968, there would be more than 536,000 US military personnel in Vietnam. Many of those soldiers were draftees

Struggling with Terrain

The terrain and climate in Vietnam presented unique challenges to American soldiers. Much of Vietnam's landscape is mountainous or hilly, with high peaks to the north and west. Some of the hilly areas had been cleared for farming, much of the landscape was covered in dense tropical jungle. The nation's location near the equator and the dense jungle contributed to conditions that were hot and humid. Vietnam also regularly experiences long periods of intense seasonal rainstorms, called monsoons. Soldiers would have to deal with the problems that these conditions caused, including malfunctioning equipment, heat-related illnesses, and daily discomfort caused by carrying equipment and wearing uniforms that were poorly designed for such warm conditions.

The North Vietnamese and Viet Cong fighters, however, were used to the climate. They also knew and understood the terrain, giving them the ability to easily attack the Americans and then fade into the landscape without a direct confrontation. The US would have to learn how to adapt to these tactics and respond quickly to such guerrilla tactics.[4]

Operation Rolling Thunder

The first major US military operation of the Vietnam War avoided many of those problems and brought some success. Operation Rolling Thunder began on March 2, 1965. The operation consisted of a widespread bombing campaign by US planes against strategic targets in North Vietnam. Johnson had several reasons for authorizing the attack. He wanted to send a message to South Vietnam that the nation had the full support of the US He also hoped to severely damage North Vietnam's ability to move weapons and soldiers along the Ho Chi Minh Trail to help the Viet Cong forces, while hurting the North Vietnamese army's morale.

The bombing campaign lasted until October 1968, eventually growing to include nearly all of North Vietnam, including air fields, power plants, factories, and military facilities. The campaign had some success in destroying important targets, but the results were mixed in the end. While supporters of the bombings believed that the effort came close to crippling North Vietnam's military, critics point out that North Vietnamese forces managed to shoot down hundreds of planes, despite having a tiny air force.[5]

Important government targets were left alone because the planes were forbidden from bombing in the capital city of Hanoi. The factories that were destroyed also did little to harm North Vietnam's war effort, since so much of their fighting was done through low-tech guerilla operations. The North Vietnamese army and Viet Cong fighters quickly learned to adapt to the bombardments, using the carefully constructed tunnels and bunkers along the Ho Chi Minh Trail as shelters. Later, American military commanders also failed to coordinate the bombings with the maneuvers of ground forces.

Operation Rolling Thunder was the kind of military campaign that General Westmoreland liked. Westmoreland's key strategy in Vietnam was one of victory through attrition. He believed that the US could use its superior weapons and troop numbers to wear down the North Vietnamese and Viet Cong fighters. Johnson also believed this strategy would work. Throughout the war, McNamara would present Johnson with statistics that showed the US forces were inflicting far more casualties than they were taking.[6]

Fighting on the Ground

Johnson continued to send troops into Vietnam. Two more battalions of Marines went over, and Johnson authorized soldiers to go on patrols into the countryside in an attempt to hunt down Viet Cong guerrillas. These operations came to be known as search-and-destroy missions. Small groups of soldiers would move through South Vietnam's villages and jungle terrain, looking for Viet Cong fighters.

The American soldiers had far better weapons and equipment than the North Vietnamese or the Viet Cong fighters. From the air, the US could use enormous B-52 bombers to drop explosives and toxic jungle-killing herbicides throughout Vietnam. Smaller reconnaissance planes could scout out enemy positions, while helicopters gave the Americans a rapid and unpredictable means of attack. Warships and patrol boats cruised the rivers and coastline. Big trucks could haul the heavy US artillery along the newly-built roads that the Americans had carved out across the countryside. The soldiers themselves were equipped with fully automatic machine guns, protective helmets, explosives, and radios that they could use to communicate with other soldiers.

The US advantage in weaponry did not translate into success in the field. The Viet Cong fighters knew the countryside well. Most of the American soldiers they faced found it to be a confusing and inhospitable place, filled with biting insects and deadly wildlife such as tigers and vipers. The days could be unbearable hot, while dropping nighttime temperatures might leave them shivering. The Viet Cong could use their own deep knowledge of the countryside and the discomfort and confusion of the Americans to pull of swift attacks and ambushes. They hoped to wear down the US troops in much the same way that General Westmoreland hoped to wear down North Vietnam.[7]

The plan to wage a war of attrition against North Vietnam had several serious flaws. North Vietnam was perfectly willing to send in as many fighters as necessary to

Fighting in South Vietnam's countryside often put US forces in unfamiliar situations, such as these soldiers taking cover in a flooded rice paddy.

win the war, regardless of the loss of life. The nation was fully committed to the cause of uniting the two Vietnams.

The situation was more complicated for the US Johnson's administration used a strategy called the Individual Rotation Policy to keep troop numbers high. Many of the soldiers who were sent to Vietnam had been drafted. While the military draft was an accepted policy in the US in the years following World War II, Johnson had to drastically increase the size of the draft in order to get enough soldiers to fight North Vietnam and the Viet Cong. Training for most draftees lasted just four to six months before they were shipped out to Vietnam.

Congress had passed a law that limited the amount of time that a draftee could serve in the military to two years. Factoring in travel time, training, and leave time, most of the drafted soldiers served for only about a year in Vietnam before they were sent home. This meant by the time they had become experienced and seasoned fighters, it was time for them to return to civilian life, or "rotate out." By expanding the draft and keeping fresh draftees cycling in to Vietnam, Johnson was able to keep troop numbers high without fully committing the US military to the war effort.[8]

The Individual Rotation Policy was deeply flawed, even beyond the minimal training that the draftees received. The short period of time that the soldiers spent in Vietnam meant that army units often lacked real unity. Newly-arrived soldiers were often thrown in among hardened veterans who had little time or patience to help them adjust to the fighting around them. This often left new recruits feeling isolated, on top of the fear and anxiety that comes with fighting. The veterans had already gone through what the new recruits were experiencing and were counting down time until they could rotate out and return home.

This reliance on drafted soldiers who were always rotating out meant that by the time the soldiers were experienced enough to become leaders within units, they were sent home. The strategy also gave soldiers little time to bond and learn how to work together as well as they might if they had trained together.

The policy had critics within the administration. Army Chief of Staff General Harold Johnson (no relation to Lyndon Johnson) believed that the US needed 1 million troops on the ground. This would mean calling up the

National Guard and Reserve forces. Members of these two forces are not full-time military personnel, but they have much more experience than draftees. Reservists and National Guard units train together on a regular basis, ship out together to fight, and know how to work together before entering combat. Harold Johnson believed that the quality of the military force in Vietnam would go down dramatically if the Reserve and National Guard did not enter the war.[9]

President Johnson was against the idea of sending the nation's reserve forces to Vietnam. He believed that bringing these soldiers into the war would turn public opinion against the war at a time when more people were already beginning to question the US presence in Vietnam. He believed that mobilizing the Reserves and the National Guard would lead to debates in Congress over whether the US should be fighting in Vietnam at all. Such a debate might completely derail his War on Poverty programs. McNamara also opposed the idea, though many of the highest-ranking military leaders believed it would be necessary. Instead, McNamara pushed to expand the draft. This was done again and again.

Active debates were held about whether to make each draftee's tour of duty fifteen months instead of twelve, in an effort to improve the effectiveness of units and drastically reduce the number of replacement soldiers needed. The idea was rejected on the basis that serving a longer tour of duty in Vietnam's uncomfortable climate would inflict psychological harm on the soldiers and that morale would get worse. General Westmoreland himself spoke up in favor of keeping the tours at twelve months.[10]

Resisting the Draft

People who have no desire to fight have been resisting military drafts since the beginning of the Spanish-American War in 1898. Often, the draft resisters were relatively few in numbers. That changed during the Vietnam War, when opposition to the fighting swept through college campuses and so many young men refused to go and fight that the Selective Service had a hard time meeting its quotas.

Resistance took many forms. Some men simply refused to show up when they were told that they had been drafted. Some filed as conscientious objectors, meaning that they claimed to have a religious or moral opposition to violence that prevented them from fighting. Others claimed to have disabilities that made them unable to fight. Networks of antiwar activists and draft resisters also sneaked draftees across the border and into Canada, where they would be safe from having to join the war effort. By the time the war ended, about 206,000 men had dodged the draft.[11]

Johnson would continue to ignore recommendations to call up the Reserve and National Guard until 1968. By that point, public opinion was turning against the war and Johnson's own approval ratings had fallen sharply.

Allies in the Field

The alliance between the US and South Vietnam remained intact. The political and social chaos that continued to roil through South Vietnam constantly complicated the relationship. Much of South Vietnam's population remained hostile to their government. Many joined the Viet Cong's war against the American forces, seeing them as yet another occupying military force that was doing the bidding of a corrupt government.

The continuing instability in South Vietnam did not help this perception, or the US alliance with South Vietnam. The succession of coups that had followed Diem's overthrow only provided more opportunities for corrupt officials to grab power and wealth. At the same time, they kept increasing the size of the South Vietnamese army, which had about 820,000 soldiers when the US reached its peak troop levels in 1968. The South Vietnamese had much more to lose in the war than the US soldiers, since their homes and the lives of their families were at stake.

The US was not the only country with troops fighting in Vietnam. Several other countries with anticommunist governments also sent soldiers to keep South Vietnam out of communist hands. Several nations had joined in a treaty with South Vietnam called the South East Asia Treaty Organization (SEATO). In addition to South Vietnam and the United States, the group included Australia, New Zealand, South Korea, Thailand, the Philippines, the Kingdom of Laos, the Khmer Republic (Cambodia), and the Republic of China (Taiwan).

Not all of those countries sent soldiers to fight in Vietnam, but some made important contributions in terms of personnel. South Korea, Australia, the Philippines, Thailand, and New Zealand all sent soldiers. South Korea made the biggest contribution, with fifty thousand troops in South Vietnam in 1968. Like the United States,

Members of the Royal Australian Air Force arrive in Saigon to help with the war effort by transporting soldiers and supplies into combat areas in South Vietnam.

these nations believed in the Domino Theory and wanted to prevent communism from spreading. They also recognized that Southeast Asia had been unstable in the years since World War II. Johnson's administration was able to convince their governments that aiding the American war effort would help stabilize the region.[12]

North Vietnam and the Viet Cong had two powerful allies—The People's Republic of China and the Soviet Union—as well as North Korea and communist fighters in Laos and Cambodia. China and the Soviet Union invested heavily in the war on the side of North Vietnam, sending money, food, equipment, and even some military advisors.

The Soviet Union remained deeply involved through the war's end, while China scaled back its aid to North Vietnam in the late 1960s.

Johnson's Plans

Even with American troops actively fighting and dying in Vietnam, Johnson continued to steer a middle course between the hawks and the doves in the Senate. The doves were already upset that the US had gotten so involved in the war. They wanted to end all American involvement in Vietnam. They pushed for Johnson to broker a peace between North Vietnam and South Vietnam, and to create an agreement that would reunite the two parts of the country under a government that was neutral to communism. Remarkably, Vice President Hubert Humphrey was one of the doves pushing for peace.

The hawks wanted Johnson to devote more firepower and more soldiers to the war effort. They believed that North Vietnam must be forced into submission and that the US must keep the communists from taking control of South Vietnam at all costs. They wanted Johnson to threaten to use nuclear weapons against North Vietnam, bomb Hanoi and other cities with large populations, and even consider a full-scale invasion of North Vietnam.

Johnson's middle path consisted of the ongoing bombing campaigns against North Vietnam and extensive military actions throughout South Vietnam. He took a posture of defending South Vietnam and maintained high numbers of soldiers in the country to show the North Vietnamese that the US could not be defeated. This followed Westmoreland's strategy of a war of attrition.[13]

The War and Congress

Congress had given Johnson broad powers to fight the war in Vietnam as he saw fit through the Gulf of Tonkin Resolution. As the war progressed and more American troops were sent to fight, support among members of Congress waned. Vice President Humphrey even advised Johnson to start winding the war effort down after Johnson started his second term in 1965. He was no longer committed to maintaining Kennedy's policies, and would not have to worry about his political opponents criticizing him for appearing weak as he withdrew US forces. Johnson had ignored this advice when he started sending in ground forces that spring. He would soon start paying a heavy political price.

Johnson knew that he needed the support of Congress to keep up with the war effort. Once the troops were on the ground and fighting, he believed that Congress would continue to pay for the war. He also believed that most of the members of Congress would continue to publicly support the war for as long as it lasted, though he worried that some of this support might be reluctant and based on a fear that their constituents might view opposition to the war as unpatriotic.

As the war dragged on and US troops started suffering heavy losses, the doves began more actively questioning Johnson's reasons for increasing the draft and doubting the military strategies being used. Serious debates began taking place between the hawks and the doves in Congress. Johnson had not wanted the war to distract attention from his domestic programs, but that was beginning to happen as the doves become more vocal.

Senator James Fulbright, a Democrat from Arkansas, led the Senate Foreign Relations Committee. He had voted for the Gulf of Tonkin Resolution—in fact, he had been a sponsor of the bill. Fulbright became more skeptical of the war as time passed and Johnson failed to show restraint in the number of soldiers he sent to Vietnam. By September of 1965, Fulbright had begun to see the Vietnam War as a mistake and started speaking out against the war. In 1966, his Foreign Relations Committee began holding hearings on how the war was being conducted. The hearings were shown on television, which was rare at that time. He also made several highly critical public remarks. He also published a book titled *The Arrogance of Power*, in which he criticized the justifications for the war and Congress's unwillingness to set limits on Johnson's power to carry out the conflict.[14]

Johnson felt betrayed by Fulbright and came to resent him. He believed that the criticisms from Fulbright—whom Johnson started calling "Senator Halfbright" in private—would open the war up to criticisms from the media and turn public support against the war effort.

Johnson carefully controlled the information that reporters received about the war from the White House. Early on in the war, he was a master at manipulating coverage from newspapers, television networks, and radio stations. He believed that criticism of the war from the media would hurt the war effort and did his best to keep any bad news out of the headlines. He and his press aides would avoid tricky subjects such as US losses by saying they couldn't answer questions on those topics because of national security. He would also identify reporters who were friendly to his administration and get them to ask certain questions that would help him paint the war effort in a positive light. Johnson also pressured newspapers and magazines to publish opinion columns that supported the war. He made life difficult for unfriendly reporters by refusing to answer their questions or give interviews.

When the television networks began showing Fulbright's hearings, reporters began covering them. This meant that stories about people questioning the war began showing up on television and in newspapers. Coverage of the war from

CBS News reporter Dan Rather comes under enemy fire while with American soldiers in Vietnam. Coverage of the fighting dominated nightly news broadcasts in the United States.

> **"I am not prepared to risk the security—indeed, the survival—of this American Nation on mere hope and wishful thinking. I am convinced that by seeing this struggle through now, we are greatly reducing the chances of a much larger war—perhaps a nuclear war. I would rather stand in Vietnam, in our time, and by meeting this danger now, and facing up to it, thereby reduce the danger for our children and for our grandchildren."**
>
> —*Lyndon Johnson, addressing the National Legislative Conference in San Antonio, Texas, September 29, 1967*[15]

Vietnam also became more than a daily tally of air strikes and the numbers of North Vietnamese and Viet Cong soldiers who were killed or captured. Journalists began showing acts of violence committed by US troops against civilians, as well as the physical and emotional toll that the war was taking on American soldiers.

Even Defense Secretary Robert McNamara was beginning to believe that the war was getting out of hand. In November 1967, he sent a memo advising Johnson to stop sending more troops, start handing the ground fighting over to South Vietnam's army, and end the bombing in North Vietnam. Johnson refused the advice. A short time later, McNamara announced that he would be resigning from his post in February of 1968. With McNamara leaving, Johnson would lose one of his strongest supporters of the war.[16]

The Domestic Agenda

Johnson's ambitious goals for transforming US society had gotten off to a good start early in his second term, but the war drew attention away from his plans. Congress had ratified the Twenty-Fourth Amendment to the Constitution in January of 1964, which made it illegal for people to have to pay in order to vote—a practice that was often used to keep poor African Americans from voting. His signing of the Civil Rights Act of 1964 and the Economic Opportunity Act later that year were key to his civil rights efforts and the beginning of his War on Poverty.

In March of 1965, he introduced the Voting Rights Act in Congress, which would guarantee that African Americans and other minorities would have the right to vote. The actions of civil rights leader Martin Luther King, Jr. and others helped encourage Johnson to go ahead with the legislation despite his worries that it might hold up his other objectives. The bill was passed in August of that year and made it illegal to keep registered voters from voting. It also gave the US Justice Department the authority to act in places where discriminatory voting practices were being used.

Later in 1965, he signed several important bills related to his War on Poverty into law. One was the Elementary and Secondary Education Act. The law provides funds for public elementary schools and high schools, while emphasizing equal access to schools and high levels of accountability. Another bill created the Medicare and Medicaid program, which provide medical services to the elderly and low-income people.

Johnson made strides in other areas, as well. he managed to get Congress to pass protections against air and water pollution, as well as a highway beautification bill that encouraged the planting of trees and flowers along major roadways. While these landmark achievements help many people, much of the rest of Johnson's presidency was taken up by the Vietnam war.

SPINNING OUT OF CONTROL

Even after building up the US presence in South Vietnam, Johnson wanted to get the US out of Vietnam. The war was taking up more and more of his attention. He was bothered by the increasing number of US casualties and by growing public opposition to the war. Both North Vietnam and the United States tried to start peace negotiations, but neither side could agree on terms. Protests against the war were becoming common on US college campuses and in large cities as public opposition to the war grew, especially among younger people who were at the age where they could be drafted. In 1965, the survey company Gallup Polls conducted an opinion poll that found that 25 percent of Americans thought it was a mistake to send soldier to Vietnam. By 1971—after Johnson left office—that number had grown to 61 percent who saw the war as a mistake.[1]

The US was roiling with tension. Despite the passage of the Civil Rights Act of 1965, race relations had not improved. Some segregationist leaders—including Alabama governor George Wallace—tried to block African Americans from exercising their rights. Other racists used violence as they had in the past, threatening, intimidating, and even murdering civil rights activists. Martin Luther King Jr. himself was murdered in Memphis on April 4, 1968. Violence also swept through major American cities during Johnson's presidency as the result of racial tension in places such as Los Angeles's Watts neighborhood in 1965, Cleveland, Ohio, in 1966 Detroit, Michigan, in 1967, and Washington, DC, and Baltimore, Maryland, in 1968.

Skepticism and Resistance

The unpopularity of the war led to increasing resistance to the war effort in the US There had been protests against US military involvement in Vietnam going back to 1964, particularly on college campuses. The protest movement kept growing as the war dragged on. The protests took many forms. Protesters marched, staged "sit-ins" in public buildings, and gathered in parks. The protesters came from all walks of life. Many were students, but some were parents, veterans who opposed wars, members of nonviolent religious groups, civil rights activists, and members of the counterculture. In some cases, they clashed with police.

Johnson was bothered by the protesters, and felt that they were damaging troop morale and hurting the war effort. He was sensitive to the criticisms that the US should not be in Vietnam. He also became paranoid that communist activists were influencing the protests in an effort to undermine the war effort. In 1967, he even had the CIA

Some of the protests that took place against the Vietnam War drew huge numbers of people. More than 100,000 people took part in this rally in New York City, for instance.

investigate and track about thirty-five thousand antiwar protesters who had shown up at a rally at the Pentagon.

His administration was also bothered by the conduct of the war and the enormous cost. Newly appointed secretary of defense Clark Clifford believed that sending in more troops would be a mistake and that the war strategy had to be reconsidered, since the war of attrition effort was not working. He pulled together some of Johnson's most trusted advisors, as well as some of the leaders of the Democratic Party. Together, they were able to convince Johnson to cap the number of soldiers in Vietnam at just over 500,000. They also urged him to seek a peace agreement with North Vietnam.[2]

Heavy Losses

US casualties in the war increased steadily as more soldiers became involved in the fighting. Only 122 Americans were killed in Vietnam in 1963. The number rose to 216 1964, the year of the Gulf of Tonkin Incident, and to 1,928 in in 1965. The casualty rate intensified further, with 6,350 Americans killed in 1966 and 11,363 in 1967. The US experienced its biggest loss of lives of the entire war in 1968, Johnson's last year as president, when 16,899 American personnel were killed. The number of casualties declined steadily after Johnson left office. By the end of the war, 58,220 US military personnel had lost their lives in the war.[3] About 153,303 were wounded during the length of US involvement.[4]

The war was unlike any that the United States had fought before. There were very few large-scale battles. For the most part, fighting took place between small groups of soldiers and North Vietnamese or Viet Cong fighters. The US adapted as well as possible to the guerrilla warfare tactics of the Viet Cong, but lacked the knowledge of the countryside that the soldiers needed to press their advantage. It was too hard to fight an enemy that could attack in one instant and vanish in the next.

Many US soldiers were deeply affected by the things they saw and did in Vietnam. The fighting between the North Vietnamese, the Viet Cong, and the South Vietnamese could be deeply personal, and atrocities against both soldiers and civilians frequently happened. American soldiers The stress of combat, the desire for revenge against an enemy that only rarely fought out in

US Marines fight in the city of Hue against the North Vietnamese. The stress of fighting an enemy that seldom attacked in the open put a strain on American troops.

the open, and the inability to recognize an enemy fighter from a civilian led some US soldiers to commit horrible acts in Vietnam. Villages were destroyed and civilians killed in some instances. While American soldiers often formed deep bonds with others in their units, those bonds quickly disappeared as new troops cycled in and veterans cycled out.

Still, the American forces and their allies were able to fight the Viet Cong and the North Vietnamese to a draw up until January of 1968. That month, the US and its allies prepared for an unofficial cease-fire during the three-day Tet holiday. Tet marks the beginning of the lunar new year and is a traditional Vietnamese celebration. During the war, it typically meant a short break from the fighting as Vietnamese soldiers observed the holiday. But in 1968, Ho Chi Minh planned for the North Vietnamese forces and the Viet Cong to launch attacks throughout the country.

The Tet Offensive, as the attacks were later called, began on January 30 and caught the US completely by surprise. The Viet Cong and North Vietnamese forces struck against places with a heavy concentration of American forces, including the cities of Hue and Saigon. Surprised American soldiers were pushed back by the fierceness of the attacks and lost territory. The outer defenses at the US Embassy in Saigon were even breached, though those attackers were forced to retreat.[5]

The Tet Offensive had a chilling effect on the war effort in the US, even though American forces were able to regain the territory they lost in the fighting. Public opinion of Johnson's handling of the war fell, as did his approval ratings. The well-respected CBS News reporter and anchorman Walter Cronkite, who had previously been supportive of the war effort, became openly critical after visiting Vietnam in the wake of the Tet Offensive. Johnson saw the loss of Cronkite's support as a major blow.

The Tet Offensive was only one major attack from North Vietnam that year. Similar attacks were carried out over a longer period of time in May and August of 1968. The US was again able to regain its lost territory, but the stress of the attacks on American soldiers was significant. In March of 1968, a company of soldiers from the 23rd Infantry Division massacred as many as 504 unarmed

The Tet Offensive was a major blow to US efforts in Vietnam. The costly attacks forced American troops to recapture territory that had been overrun by communist forces.

The Execution of Nguyễn Văn Lém

Photojournalist Eddie Adams managed to capture the horror and brutality of the Vietnam War in a famous 1968 photo of South Vietnamese army general Nguyen Ngoc Loan killing a suspect named Nguyễn Văn Lém in the middle of a street in Saigon. Adams had been passing by when he saw the general asking questions while pointing a gun at the man's head. Adams raised his camera and took a picture, thinking he would get a photo of an interrogation. Instead, the general shot the man in the head, killing him.

Adams's photo, taken at the moment that the gun was fired, became a famous symbol used by antiwar demonstrators who protested against the fighting. Adams himself never came to terms with this use of his image, believing that it only told part of the story.[7]

civilians in two hamlets called My Lai and My Khe. Many of the villagers were women and children, and some had been tortured. Unlike the Tet Offensive, Johnson's administration was able to cover up the brutal war crimes. The media did not learn about the massacre until 1969, when Johnson was no longer president.[6]

Working Toward Peace

In 1968, The United States and North Vietnam were finally able to agree to peace talks. There had been efforts from both the US and North Vietnam to open discussions of a truce, but they were always rejected for one reason or another. North Vietnam wanted a complete US withdrawal from Vietnam and the nation to be reunified under a government that both North and South Vietnam could agree on. The US government wanted a way out of th war without admitting defeat and a guarantee that South Vietnam would be able to decide whether or not to reunify with North Vietnam.

After the Tet Offensive, President Johnson was willing to take whatever steps were necessary to put an end to the costly war. In March of 1968, he halted the Operation Rolling Thunder bombing campaign, hoping to encourage North Vietnam to join in peace talks. The talks finally began that May, with representatives from both countries meeting in Paris, France. North Vietnam sent former Foreign Minister Xuan Thuy, while the United States was represented by Ambassador W. Averell Harriman.

As the talks opened, there was a great deal of hope that a peace agreement could be reached quickly. Instead, the talks became weekly meetings, as the US and North Vietnam both refused to change their conditions for peace. The same positions and demands were repeated, over and over.[8]

Abandoning the Election

Johnson announced the pause in the bombing of North Vietnam and the planned peace talks on March 31, 1968. He also announced that he was going to end his election campaign. Many people were caught by surprise by the announcement.

"Tonight, I have ordered our aircraft and our naval vessels to make no attacks on North Vietnam, except in the area north of the demilitarized zone where the continuing enemy buildup directly threatens allied forward positions and where the movements of their troops and supplies are clearly related to that threat."

—*Lyndon Johnson, in a televised address to the American people, March 31, 1968*[9]

In truth, Johnson was worn down by Vietnam. Johnson's moods had always shifted to extremes, as he would be friendly and cheerful for days before falling into a gloomy period. The gloomy days far outnumbered the cheerful ones as the war dragged on, and his health suffered. Politically, his poll numbers had fallen to very low levels. Even if he was able to win the Democratic Party's nomination, he might not be able to defeat the Republican candidate, who turned out to be Richard Nixon.

Apart from racial tensions and protests over the war, Johnson faced several other problems at home. He had continued the war effort without ever asking Congress to raise taxes, while also spending heavily on his domestic programs. The economy suffered as a result. The price of goods went up and workers in several industries went on strike for better pay and working conditions. Fighting the war was extremely expensive—it cost $35 billion in 1967. However, Johnson did not want to cut spending at home or make people pay higher taxes, both of which would have damaged his popularity and may have lost him support in Congress.

Johnson faced serious challenges for the Democratic Party nomination from Senator Eugene McCarthy. McCarthy was running a strongly antiwar campaign and had energized antiwar activists. He had been a longtime critic of Johnson in the Senate and had begun his presidential campaign in 1967 with the hope of turning the Democratic Party against the war. He was considered a long shot candidate at first, but on March 12 he finished the New Hampshire primary very strongly with 42 percent of the vote, while Johnson had 49 percent.

Senator Robert Kennedy had announced earlier that he would not run for president and had stated he would support Johnson. Kennedy had remained popular after his election to the Senate, and decided to enter the presidential race after seeing how close Johnson came to losing a primary to the relatively unknown McCarthy. Kennedy had proposed plans to end the war in Vietnam[10]

The narrow primary victory over McCarthy and Kennedy's move to enter the race helped Johnson make up his mind to quit the race. With Johnson's encouragement and promise of support, Vice President Hubert Humphrey entered the race on April 27. Johnson hoped to help Humphrey win by securing peace in Vietnam before the election.

The Presidential Race

The presidential election that year was marked by tragedy and unusual developments, even going beyond Johnson's decision to leave the race. Kennedy, who was running a very tight race against McCarthy, was shot and fatally wounded on June 5, just hours after winning the California primary. He died the next day. He had been a charismatic candidate, and his death threw the Democratic Party into confusion. Some Democrats who had backed him went over to support McCarthy. Others supported Humphrey, who was more of an establishment candidate.

Humphrey himself had been opposed to the war while he was in the Senate and did not agree with Johnson's policy of escalation. Johnson, however, had him promise to maintain the administration's Vietnam policies. In return, Johnson would throw his still-substantial support behind Humphrey. In the end, Humphrey was able to win the nomination. However, the announcement that he would follow Johnson's policies would later hurt him.[11]

Former vice president and US senator Richard Nixon won the Republican Party nomination. Nixon, who had narrowly lost his own presidential bid in 1960 to John F. Kennedy, won the nomination against Michigan governor George Romney, New York governor Nelson Rockefeller, California governor Ronald Reagan, and US senator Charles Percy of Illinois.

During the presidential campaign, Nixon was able to use Johnson's Vietnam strategy against Humphrey in the election. Nixon also promised to bring the war to an end, though he had supported US involvement when he was in the Senate and offered few details about how that would happen. Johnson himself kept Nixon informed of developments in the war. At the same time, Nixon worked to undermine Johnson's peace efforts.

In October of 1968, the United States, North Vietnam, and South Vietnam were very close to finalizing an agreement that would stop the fighting. At that time, Nixon and Humphrey were very close in the polls. During the talks, Nixon sent messages through one of his aides to South Vietnam's ambassador to encourage him to refuse a peace deal. The negotiations fell through and the war continued. Johnson found out about Nixon's interference but did not act on the information, though the act of going around the President to halt peace talks could be treason. Humphrey also found out, but decided not to publicize the information out of fear of creating a crisis. In the end, Nixon was elected by a very narrow margin, with 43.2 percent of the vote to 42.7 percent for Humphrey. Johnson had failed to secure the peace that he wanted in Vietnam.[12]

PASSING THE BATON

Nixon's swearing in ceremony in January of 1969 would mark Johnson's exit from politics after a career as an elected official that spanned thirty years. It wasn't a change that came easily for him. Even after declaring that he would leave the 1968 presidential race, he hinted to stage a dramatic reentry at the Democratic National Convention and take the nomination in response to Humphrey's attempts to distance himself from Johnson's Vietnam policies.[1]

Nixon had been suspicious of the 1968 peace talks, believing that they were simply a way for Johnson to boost Humphrey in the polls. Even after Humphrey's defeat, Johnson still worked tirelessly to bring South Vietnam to the negotiating table and end the war. The war's enormous cost in lives and resources had taken a heavy toll on him, especially as public opinion turned against the war. He did not want his legacy to be a war that dragged on for years with nothing to show for it. However, his administration's attempts to bring about an end to the war were marred by petty disagreements over small details such as the shape of the conference table. Nixon's interference did not help, though South Vietnam had been reluctant to participate in the peace talks. By the time Johnson left office, more than thirty-one thousand Americans had died in Vietnam.[2]

Nixon Takes Over

Richard Nixon was sworn in as the thirty-seventh president of the United States on January 20, 1969. Nixon had promised throughout his campaign that he would change America's Vietnam War strategy. He called his plan

Richard M. Nixon had won the 1968 presidential election by promising a new direction in Vietnam. However, it still took him five years to end the war.

"Vietnamization," and it involved the steady transfer of responsibility for the war to South Vietnam. At the same time, he planned to reduce US troop levels and continue peace talks. Rather than simply ending the war by withdrawing US forces, Nixon wanted to achieve "peace with honor" and arrange an exit without having to admit defeat. This desire was similar to Johnson's own goals.[1]

The Vietnamization plan was introduced in March of 1969 and included the gradual phasing out of the more than 475,000 US troops still in South Vietnam. It also called for US forces to give South Vietnamese forces the equipment and training they needed to fully take over fighting. He announced the plan on television on November 3, 1969, referring to it as an alternative to Johnson's "Americanization" of the war in which the US became more deeply involved. [2]

Nixon accomplished his Vietnamization goal, though it took longer than he may have expected. Troop levels dropped to 334,600 in 1970, to 156,8000 in 1971, 24,200 in 1972, and just 50 in 1973. The US continued to experience casualties, and about 22,000 American military personnel died in Vietnam while Nixon was in office.[3]

At the same time that he was drawing these numbers down, Nixon was increasing the US military presence in other parts of Southeast Asia while encouraging Secretary of State Henry Kissinger to hold secret peace talks with North Vietnam. In 1970, Nixon ordered the military to carry out secret bombing missions and a ground invasion in Cambodia in an effort to eliminate North Vietnamese forces there.

Part of Nixon's war plan involved fighting against North Vietnamese soldiers who had crossed into Cambodia, which was technically neutral in the war.

Even as the US military presence in Vietnam declined, Americans were turning more strongly against the war. The revelation of the My Lai massacre in the spring of 1969 and news of the secret bombings and invasion of Cambodia the following year helped fuel protests across the country. The counterculture movement was in full bloom in 1969, and Nixon's policies in Vietnam looked very similar to Johnson's to many of its members.

The Kent State Massacre

Shortly after Nixon announced the invasion of Cambodia by American forces on April 30, 1970, protests broke out on campuses throughout the US. The protests on the campus of Kent State University grew out of control, as a riot broke out and a building was set on fire. The Ohio National Guard was called in to restore order, and a big antiwar rally planned for May 4 was banned by the school administration. Protesters ignored the ban and gathered anyway.

The results were tragic. The guardsmen ordered the crowd to leave and fired tear gas into the crowd to make them go away. Some of the protesters threw the gas canisters back at the guardsmen, along with rocks and sticks. Some of the guardsmen then began firing their weapons at the unarmed protesters, who fled in horror. By the time the shooting was over, four protesters had been killed and nine others wounded. The incident made many antiwar activists even more determined to end the war.[4]

Johnson in Retirement

While Nixon dealt with the war in Vietnam and unrest at home, Johnson was retired and living on the family ranch in Texas, which he had purchased in 1951. There, he happily worked on projects such as installing a new irrigation system and building up his herd of cattle. He made it clear from the start of his retirement that he did not want to talk to the press or be in the public eye. He blamed the media for what he saw as constant criticism of his policies, without recognizing his achievements. Exhausted by his time in office and ailing from heart problems, he largely avoided public appearances.[5]

He dedicated much of his first year out of office to completing his autobiography—which was completed in 1971 under the title *The Vantage Point: Perspectives of the Presidency 1963–1969*—and overseeing the construction of the Lyndon Baines Johnson Presidential Library and museum, on the campus of the University of Texas at Austin. The library contains the university's Lyndon Baines Johnson School of Public Affairs and an astonishing thirty-one million documents that Johnson had collected throughout his career in politics.

He stayed up to date on developments in Washington. Secretary of State Henry Kissinger regularly briefed Johnson on what was happening politically. Johnson largely approved of Nixon's policies in Vietnam, though he worried that the US was leaving before South Vietnam would truly be able to defend itself. He reflected on his own mistakes in the war, especially his failure to send in troops soon enough to make a real difference.[6]

> **"To begin with, Kennedy should have had more than eighteen thousand military advisers there in the early 1960s. And then I made the situation worse by waiting eighteen months before putting more men in. By then, the war was almost lost. Another mistake was not instituting censorship—not to cover up mistakes, but to prevent the other side from knowing what we were going to do next. My God, you can't fight a war by watching it every night on television."**
>
> —*Lyndon Johnson, in conversation with Leo Janos in 1971* [7]

Johnson had very little involvement in the 1972 presidential election, as his health rapidly grew worse following a serious heart attack that April. His former vice president, Hubert Humphrey, was among the candidates running for the Democratic Party's nomination. The relationship between Johnson and Humphrey was icy, and Johnson chose instead to endorse former North Carolina Governor (and future Senator) Terry Sanford, who shared Johnson's interest in civil rights and fighting poverty. Sanford received little support at the Democratic National Convention. Senator George McGovern won the nomination and went on to lose the presidential race to Nixon in a landslide.[8]

Johnson died on January 22, 1973, of a heart attack. In the days shortly before his death, he had heard that Nixon was on the verge of ending the war in Vietnam. He had already put an assistant to work on writing a statement to mark the occasion.

Brokered Peace

Nixon did finally secure the end of US involvement. On January 27, 1973, the Paris Peace Accords were signed. The agreement marked the conclusion of the talks that Johnson had started in 1968, when the sides concerned couldn't agree on the shape of the table. The Paris Peace Accords set August 15, 1973, as the day that the United States would end all combat operations in Vietnam.

The war was far from over, however. Nixon's Vietnamization plan had helped bulk up South Vietnam's army to 1,048,000 by the end of 1972. South Vietnam would keep fighting against the Viet Cong, but without direct US military support. The United States did continue to provide aid to South Vietnam's army in the hope that it would withstand the communist forces. That hope was in vain. Fighting continued for nearly two more years, until North Vietnam launched a full-scale invasion of South Vietnam in January of 1975.

By April of 1975, Saigon was surrounded by North Vietnamese soldiers and Nixon had left office after resigning in disgrace. President Gerald Ford, Nixon's vice president at the time of his resignation, became the fifth US president to have to deal with the conflict in Vietnam. By that time, South Vietnam's government had completely collapsed and North Vietnam controlled almost the entire country.

Ford declared the war to be over on April 23, 1975. He also ordered all of the US government staff members and

The final US evacuation from Saigon was extremely chaotic, as government staffers were airlifted from their embassy by helicopter to be transported to an aircraft carrier.

American citizens to leave Saigon as soon as possible. US personnel staged their final evacuation by helicopter from the roof of the US Embassy building as North Vietnamese soldiers took control of the city. Vietnam was finally united, but under a communist government.[9]

CONCLUSION

Johnson's legacy as a president is split between his strong civil rights record and his social programs on one side and the war in Vietnam on the other. While he showed remarkable poise in guiding the nation through the assassination of John F. Kennedy, he was unable to find a way out of the conflict that Kennedy had hoped to avoid. His mastery of the Senate resulted in the passage of strong anti-discrimination laws and brought new opportunities to millions of impoverished Americans. At the same time, he committed hundreds of thousands of young men to fighting in a war thousands of miles away.

The war in Vietnam had an enormous cost for all sides. The US lost a total of 58,220 personnel during the war, including deaths by accident and those who were presumed dead but whose bodies were never recovered. More than 100,000 were wounded, and many more bore deep psychological scars from the horrors they witnessed.

For the Vietnamese, the numbers were staggering. In 1995, Vietnam released estimates showing that between

1954 and 1975, a total of about two million civilians were killed on both sides. North Vietnamese military deaths totaled about 1.1 million. US estimates for South Vietnam's military casualties is between 200,000 and 250,000 killed. The landscape was altered by bombs, landmines, roads, and the chemical defoliants that the US had sprayed over the jungles. Those same chemicals were later found to cause birth defects in places where they had been used.

During and after Johnson's presidency, the war tore at the fabric of American society, as protesters voiced their disapproval in ever-growing numbers. Soldiers returning from their tours of duty were met by protesters and made to feel unwelcome. The nation's confidence suffered, as

The Vietnam Memorial in Washington, DC, is a wall that lists the names of American military personnel who died during the conflict, going all the way back to 1959.

well. The United States had the most powerful military in the world but was unable to defeat fighters who relied on very little technology and would only seldom fight out in the open.

In the aftermath of the reunification, Vietnam went on to fight other costly wars against Cambodia and China. Within the nation, people who were believed to have been loyal to South Vietnam's government were persecuted, and sometimes even arrested and killed. Millions of Vietnamese citizens fled the country in the late 1970s and early 1980s. Many traveled by rickety boats to places such as Australia, New Zealand, and the United States, where they built new lives.

Vietnam remains a communist nation, though its relationship with the United States has gotten easier since the reestablishment of diplomatic ties in 1995. Vietnam and the US now trade freely together. The dominos that Johnson had feared did not fall.

CHRONOLOGY

1883

France establishes French Indochina.

1908

Lyndon Baines Johnson is born in Stonewall, Texas.

1919

Ho Chi Minh writes a resolution requesting that France give Vietnam more independence.

1924

Lyndon Johnson graduates from high school.

1930

Lyndon Johnson graduates from Southwest Texas State Teachers College.

1934

Lyndon Johnson marries Claudia "Lady Bird" Taylor.

1935

President Roosevelt makes Lyndon Texas's director of the National Youth Organization

1937

Johnson is elected to the US House of Representatives.

1941

Ho Chi Minh founds the Viet Minh.

1945

Vietnam declares its independence, establishing the Democratic Republic of Vietnam.

1949

Johnson wins a seat in the US Senate.

1954

The Geneva Accords arrange France's withdrawal from Vietnam and the nation's division.

1955

Lyndon Johnson becomes Senate majority leader.

1955

Ngo Dinh Diem is named prime minister of South Vietnam.

1956

France leaves Vietnam.

1958

Johnson drives Congress to pass important civil rights legislation.

1959

The first Americans are killed as a result of the Vietnam War.

1960

John F. Kennedy is elected president, with Lyndon Johnson as his vice prersident.

1962

US helicopters participate in Operation Chopper in South Vietnam.

1962

The Strategic Hamlet Program begins in South Vietnam.

1963

South Vietnam's prime minister, Ngo Dinh Diem, is deposed and assassinated.

1963

An assassin kills President Kennedy, and Johnson becomes president.

1964

President Johnson promises to follow Kennedy's plans in Vietnam.

1964

Johnson sets out his plans for a "War on Poverty."

1964

The Civil Rights Act of 1964 is signed into law.

1964

American ships are attacked in the Gulf of Tonkin, prompting the Gulf of Tonkin Resolution.

1964

Lyndon Johnson is elected to a full term as president with Hubert Humphrey as vice president.

1965

The United States begins combat operations in Vietnam with Operation Flaming Dart. The Voting Rights Act is signed.

1965

Heavy bombing of North Vietnam begins.

1966

Senator James Fulbright holds his first televised hearings on the Vietnam War.

1968

Lyndon Johnson announces that he will not run for reelection.

1968

Johnson begins peace talks with North Vietnam and South Vietnam.

1968

Richard Nixon defeats Vice President Hubert Humphrey in the presidential election.

1970

The US invades Cambodia, touching off protests.

1973

Lyndon Johnson dies at his ranch in Stonewall, Texas.

1973

The US signs the Paris Peace Accords, arranging the end of the war.

1973

The US military leaves South Vietnam.

1975

Saigon falls, and the last US personnel evacuate the city by helicopter.

CHAPTER NOTES

CHAPTER 1: GROWING INTO POLITICS

1. "A Texas Boy 'Born Into Politics,'" *New York Times*, January 23, 1973.
2. Ibid.
3. Ibid.
4. Lyndon Johnson, "Address to Congress: We Shall Overcome," March 15, 1965.
5. Miller Center of Public Affairs, University of Virginia, "Lyndon B. Johnson: Life Before the Presidency," http://millercenter.org/president/biography/lbjohnson-life-before-the-presidency.
6. Enid Nemy, "Lady Bird Johnson, Former First Lady, Dies at 94," *New York Times*, July 11, 2007.
7. Robert Dallek, *Lone Star Rising: Lyndon Johnson and His Times, 1908–1960* (New York, NY: Oxford University Press, 1991).
8. Ibid.
9. Robert A. Caro, *Means of Ascent (The Years of Lyndon Johnson)*. (New York, NY: Vintage Press, 1991).
10. Ibid.
11. Ibid.
12. Ibid.

CHAPTER 2: A NATION IN CONFLICT

1. Stanley Karnow, *Vietnam: A History* (New York, NY: Penguin Books, 1997).
2. Ibid.
3. Robert C. Cottrell, *Vietnam: The 17th Parallel (Arbitrary Borders)* (Philadelphia, PA: Chelsea House Publishers, 2004).
4. Ibid.
5. Margaret MacMillan, *Paris 1919: Six Months that Changed the World* (New York, NY: Random House, 2003).
6. Karnow.

7. History Matters, "Declaration of Independence of the Democratic Republic of Vietnam," September 2, 1945.
8. Karnow.
8. Karnow.

CHAPTER 3: ESCALATION IN ASIA

1. Dwight Eisenhower, "The President's News Conference," April 7, 1954, http://www.presidency.ucsb.edu/ws/?pid=10202.
2. Lieutenant General John J. Tolson. *Vietnam Studies: Air Mobility, 1961–1971* (Washington, DC: Department of the Army, 1999).
3. Peter Grose, "Vietnam Outlook Bleaker a Year After Diem's Fall," *New York Times*, November 2, 1964.
4. John F. Kennedy Presidential Library and Museum, "Vietnam, Diem, the Buddhist Crisis," https://www.jfklibrary.org/JFK/JFK-in-History/Vietnam-Diem-and-the-Buddhist-Crisis.aspx.
5. Stanley Karnow, *Vietnam: A History*.
6. Robert A. Caro, "The Transition: Lyndon Johnson and the Events in Dallas," *New Yorker*, April 2, 2012.
7. Robert Dallek, *Flawed Giant: Lyndon Johnson and His Times, 1961-1973* (New York, NY: Oxford University Press, 1998).
8. Lyndon Johnson, "First State of the Union Address," January 8, 1964, http://www.americanrhetoric.com/speeches/lbj1964stateoftheunion.htm
9. Ibid.

CHAPTER 4: ASSESSING VIETNAM

1. The American War Library, "Vietnam War Allied Troop Levels, 1960–1973," http://www.americanwarlibrary.com/vietnam/vwatl.htm
2. Robert Dallek. *Flawed Giant: Lyndon Johnson and His Times, 1961-1973*.

3. Stanley Karnow, *Vietnam: A History*.
4. Tim Weiner, "Robert S. McNamara, Architect of a Futile War, Dies at 93," *New York Times*, July 6, 2009.
5. Jack Raymond, "McNamara Tells Johnson of Gain in Vietnam War," *New York Times, March 15, 1964*.
6. Transcript of Television and Radio interview conducted by representatives of major broadcast services, March 15, 1964, http://www.presidency.ucsb.edu/ws/index.php?pid=26108
7. Karnow.
8. Central Intelligence Agency, "The Strategic Hamlet Program," July 3, 1962.
9. Irving Bernstein, *Guns or Butter: The Presidency of Lyndon Johnson* (New York, NY: Oxford University Press, 1996).
10. Dallek.
11. Ibid.

CHAPTER 5: THE MIDDLE COURSE

1. CBS News, "How Many Americans Died in Korea?" http://www.cbsnews.com/news/how-many-americans-died-in-korea/.
2. David Coleman, "LBJ's Presidential Approval Ratings, 1963–1969." History in Pieces, http://historyinpieces.com/research/lbj-presidential-approval-ratings.
3. Lyndon Johnson, "Remarks in Memorial Hall, Akron University," October 21, 1964, http://www.presidency.ucsb.edu/ws/?pid=26635
4. Ibid.
5. Pat Paterson, "The Truth About Tonkin," *Naval History Magazine*, February 2008.
6. Ibid.
7. Ibid.
8. Ibid.
9. Stanley Karnow, *Vietnam: A History*.

10. John Nichols, "Remembering the Folly of 'Blank Check' War and 'Escalation Unlimited,'" *Nation*, August 7, 2014.
11. Robert Dallek, *Flawed Giant: Lyndon Johnson and His Times, 1961-1973*.
12. Conelrad, "Daisy: The Complete History of an Infamous and Iconic Ad," http://www.conelrad.com/daisy/index.php.
13. Robert Mann, "How the 'Daisy Ad' Changed Everything About Political Advertising," Smithsonian.com, April 13, 2016, http://www.smithsonianmag.com/history/how-daisy-ad-changed-everything-about-political-advertising-180958741/
14. Karnow.

CHAPTER 6: SHIFTING MOMENTUM

1. Stanley Karnow, *Vietnam: A History*.
2. David Coleman, "LBJ's Presidential Approval Ratings, 1963–1969."
3. Selective Service System, "Induction Statistics." https://www.sss.gov/About/History-And-Records/Induction-Statistics
4. Karnow.
5. Ibid.
6. Ibid.
7. Ibid.
8. Mark Depu, "Vietnam War: The Individual Rotation Policy," *HistoryNet*, November 13, 2006, http://www.historynet.com/vietnam-war-the-individual-rotation-policy.htm.
9. Robert Dallek, *Flawed Giant: Lyndon Johnson and His Times, 1961-1973*.
10. Ibid.
11. Jesse Kindig, "Vietnam: Draft Resistance," *Antiwar and Radical History Project—Pacific Northwest*, http://depts.washington.edu/antiwar/vietnam_draft.shtml.

12. The American War Library, "Vietnam War Allied Troop Levels, 1960–1973."
13. Dallek,
14. Julien E. Zelizer, "How Congress Got Us Out of Vietnam," *American Prospect*, February 19, 2007, http://prospect.org/article/how-congress-got-us-out-vietnam.
15. Lyndon Johnson, "Address on Vietnam Before the National Legislative Conference, San Antonio, Texas," September 29, 1967, http://www.presidency.ucsb.edu/ws/index.php?pid=28460&st=Johnson&st1=.
16. Dallek.

CHAPTER 7: SPINNING OUT OF CONTROL

1. Gallup Polls, "Timeline of Polling History: Events That Shaped the United States, and the World." http://www.gallup.com/poll/9967/timeline-polling-history-events-shaped-united-states-world.aspx.
2. Robert Dallek, *Flawed Giant: Lyndon Johnson and His Times, 1961-1973*.
3. US National Archives, "Statistical Information About Casualties of the Vietnam War," https://www.archives.gov/research/military/vietnam-war/casualty-statistics.html#date.
4. US Department of Veterans Affairs, "Military Health History Pocket Card: Vietnam," https://www.va.gov/oaa/pocketcard/m-vietnam.asp.
5. Stanley Karnow, *Vietnam: A History*.
6. Dallek.
7. Margot Adler, "The Vietnam War, Through Eddie Adams's Lens," *NPR*, March 24, 2009, http://www.npr.org/2009/03/24/102112403/the-vietnam-war-through-eddie-adams-lens.
8. Dallek.

9. Lyndon Johnson, "The President's Address to the Nation Announcing Steps to Limit the War in Vietnam and Reporting His Decision Not to Seek Reelection," March 31, 1968. http://www.presidency.ucsb.edu/ws/index.php?pid=28772&st=demilitarized+zone&st1=.
10. Dallek.
11. Ibid.
12. Jason Daley, "Notes Indicate Nixon Interfered with 1968 Peace Talks," *Smithsonian.com*, January 2, 2017, http://www.smithsonianmag.com/smart-news/notes-indicate-nixon-interfered-1968-peace-talks-180961627/.

CHAPTER 8: PASSING THE BATON

1. Robert Dallek, *Flawed Giant: Lyndon Johnson and His Times, 1961-1973*.
2. Peter Baker, "Nixon Tried to Spoil Johnson's Vietnam Peace Talks in '68, Notes Show," *New York Times*, January 2, 2016.
3. Dallek.
4. Ibid.
5. The American War Library, "Vietnam War Allied Troop Levels, 1960-1973."
6. Cydney Adams, "May 4, 1970: Guardsmen Open Fire on Kent State Protesters, *CBS News*, May 4, 2016, http://www.cbsnews.com/news/on-this-day-may-4-1970-guardsmen-open-fire-on-kent-state-protesters/.
7. Dallek.
8. Leo Janos, "The Last Days of the President," *Atlantic*, July 1973, https://www.theatlantic.com/magazine/archive/1973/07/the-last-days-of-the-president/376281/.
9. Ibid.
10. Max Frankel, "McGovern Nominated on the First Ballot, and Will Run on Platform He Had Sought," *New York Times*, July 14, 1972.
11. Stanley Karnow, *Vietnam: A History*.

GLOSSARY

assassination The murder of a public figure or famous person in a surprise attack.

bombardment The heavy use of artillery over a large area, rather than an attack against a single target.

Buddhism A religion that teaches that life is full of suffering caused by desire, and that suffering ends when a person has found enlightenment through wisdom and proper conduct.

campaign A series of actions taken by a political candidate in an attempt to win an election.

communism A political system in which individuals do not own private property and class boundaries have been erased.

Congress In the US, the group of individuals elected to make laws for the entire nation, and consisting of the House of Representatives and the Senate.

corrupt Doing illegal, immoral, or dishonest things to gain power or from a position of power.

defection The conscious act of abandoning your loyalty or your duty to a person, country, or cause.

discrimination The act of treating someone differently based on something other than individual merit, such as race, gender, or place of origin.

guerrilla A fighter who engages in irregular warfare, such as sabotage or setting traps.

infrastructure A city, state, or nation's public works.

integration The act of bringing different groups of people together as equals within a society.

legislation A matter of business being considered by a representative government body, such as Congress.

monsoon In parts of Asia, a season marked by long periods of intense wind and rainfall.

peasant A class of people who work the land as small farmers or laborers.

primary An election in a state, county, or city in which voters choose candidates for the main election.

profound Great or intense; deep and meaningful.

FURTHER READING

BOOKS

Chandler, Kimberly, Ph.D., and Molly Sandling. *Exploring America in the 1960s: Our Voices Will be Heard*. Waco, TX: Prufrock Press, 2014.

Day, Meredith. *Lyndon B. Johnson* (Pivotal Presidents: Profiles in Leadership). New York, NY: Britannica Educational Publishing, 2016.

Freedman, Russell. *Vietnam: A History of the War*. New York, NY: Holiday House, 2016.

Rowell, Rebecca. *John F. Kennedy's Presidency* (Presidential Powerhouses). Minneapolis, MN: Lerner Publishing, 2017.

WEBSITES

Battlefield: Vietnam

http://www.pbs.org/battlefieldvietnam/history

Very thorough companion website to the PBS documentary series.

Lyndon Baines Johnson Presidential Library and Museum

http://www.lbjlibrary.org

Houses biographical information about President Johnson, including an archive of speeches and videos.

FILMS

LBJ: American Experience

Directed by David Grubin. PBS, 1991.

INDEX

A

assassinations, 43, 47, 49, 57, 109,

B

Bien Hoa, Vietnam, 34

C

Cambodia, 62, 78, 79, 102, 104, 111
campaigns, 15, 18, 20, 22, 27, 35, 53, 55, 58, 59, 64, 65, 67, 71, 72, 80, 95, 97, 98, 101
casualties, 56, 72, 87, 90, 102, 110
Catholicism, 27, 36, 40
Central Intelligence Agency (CIA), 32, 88
Civil Rights Act of 1964, 64, 65, 85, 87, 88
civil war, 7, 23, 25
Cold War, 7, 20, 31, 49
communism, 7, 8, 20, 23, 28, 31, 32–34, 36, 38–40, 49, 50, 52, 56, 57, 59, 65, 69, 78–80, 88, 107, 108, 111
Congress, 36, 45, 54, 55, 62–64, 75, 76, 81, 82, 85, 86, 96, 97
corruption, 34, 40, 78
coups, 41–43, 78
Cronkite, Walter, 93
Cuba, 36, 45

D

Diem, Ngo Dinh, 33, 34, 39–44, 47, 49, 52, 53, 78
discrimination, 15, 21, 22, 36, 64, 85, 109
Domino Theory, 38, 79, 111
draft, 70, 74–76, 81, 87

E

Economic Opportunity Act, 85
election, 15, 20, 32, 34, 36, 57, 63–65, 95, 97, 98, 106

F

Fulbright, James, 82, 83

G

guerrillas, 34, 39, 69, 71, 72, 91
Gulf of Tonkin, 59, 62–64, 81, 82, 90

H

Ho Chi Minh, 28, 31–34, 39, 41, 42, 50, 55, 67, 71, 72, 92
House of Representatives, 11, 15, 18—20, 54, 63

I

independence, 7, 23, 28, 31, 32, 39

J

Johnson, Claudia "Lady Bird," 16, 18
Johnson, Lyndon B.
  becomes president, 43–46
  becomes vice president, 35–39, 43
  college and early career, 12–15
  death of, 106–107
  legacy, 9, 109–111
  start in politics, 15–22
  youth, 10–12

K

Kennedy, John F., 35, 36, 38, 39, 41, 43–45, 47–50, 57, 64, 81, 97, 98, 106, 109
Kleberg, Richard, 15, 16

L

legislation, 9, 16, 21, 22, 36, 53–55, 63, 85

M

McNamara, Robert, 49, 50, 61, 67, 68, 72, 76, 84

N

National Youth Administration (NYA), 18
New Deal, 18, 20, 45, 64
Nixon, Richard, 36, 96, 98–102, 104–107

O

Operation Flaming Dart, 68

P

peasant uprising, 28

R

reunification, 27, 34, 111

S

Saigon, Vietnam, 27, 32, 38, 39, 41, 42, 49, 92, 107, 108
Senate, 19—22, 35, 54, 57, 63, 97, 98, 109
Senate Foreign Relations Committee, 82
Southwest Texas State Teachers College, 12, 13
Soviet Union, 7, 20, 36, 38, 45, 48, 49, 56, 79, 80

T

Tet Offensive, 93–95

V

Viet Cong, 34, 39, 40, 47, 49, 50, 52, 65, 67, 69, 71–74, 78, 79, 84, 91, 92, 107
Voting Rights Act, 85

W

War on Poverty, 45, 46, 62, 64, 65, 76, 85